Opportunity for all

Tackling poverty and social exclusion

Presented to Parliament by
the Secretary of State for Social Security
by Command of Her Majesty
September 1999

Cm 4445

£17.00

This publication is also available in Braille, audiocassette, and in Welsh (Cm 4445, price £17.00) from Stationery Office bookshops. A list of their bookshops is given on the back of this publication.

There are summary versions in the same formats available free of charge from:

Welfare Reform
Freepost (HA4441)
Hayes UB3 1BR

Tel: 0181 867 3201
Fax: 0181 867 3264

A service for textphone users is available on **0181 867 3217**.

The lines are open Monday to Friday, 9am–5pm. **Please quote code PSE.**

This publication and the summary version can be accessed on the internet at:
http://www.dss.gov.uk

Contents

The paintings featured in this report were created by the children of Vicarage Primary School, East Ham and St John's Meads Church of England School, Eastbourne.

Foreword

When we came into office, we inherited a country where one in five children lived in a household where no one worked, thousands left school without basic skills, and three million working-age people were out of work and had been dependent on benefits for over two years.

For many people, the past two decades have brought rising prosperity and widening opportunities. But far too many individuals, families and communities have not shared in the benefits of economic growth. And for many, disadvantage has been passed from generation to generation as children inherit poverty from their parents before passing on this debilitating legacy to their own children.

It is that injustice and waste that the Government is determined to tackle. It is morally wrong and economically foolish to allow a whole generation to be written off. You can't choose between a successful and stable economy on the one hand, and confronting poverty and its causes on the other. Fairness and enterprise go hand in hand. That is why we have set some demanding goals to make Britain a better place to live in the next century.

In particular, the Prime Minister has set out our aims of eradicating child poverty within 20 years, of confronting the waste of long-term unemployment, and of bringing deprived neighbourhoods up to the standards that the rest of Britain takes for granted – cutting crime, increasing employment, improving health and housing.

These are ambitious goals. But there is a determination across government to achieve them – through radical reform where necessary.

That means:

* making sure that **all** children are given a decent start in life and that our education system is world class;

* ensuring that our social security and employment systems play an **active** role in helping people who can work to do so, whilst protecting those who cannot;

* making sure that pensioners are given **opportunities** to enjoy active and fulfilling retirement years, and that they are given the support they need to remain in their own homes for as long as possible; and

* building thriving communities, in which **all** our citizens can enjoy a decent quality of life wherever they live, through effective, efficient and co-ordinated policies across all government agencies.

We all have a part to play in this. Government can create the economic conditions for growth, as well as providing services and investing to tackle social problems.

But the Government cannot solve problems alone. We need to work with people to encourage them to help themselves, with businesses in the regeneration process and in the drive to get people back to work. And we need to work in partnership with those with expert knowledge of particular problems and the needs of particular areas. That means building much closer links between central government and local authorities, and with voluntary sector organisations.

Our programme of constitutional reforms, bringing democratic control closer to the people, gives us the opportunity to build new partnerships between the Government and the devolved administrations to tackle poverty and social exclusion. This is an opportunity for us to learn from one another, and enhance our abilities to tackle the problems that we all face.

We face a massive task. The problems of poverty and social exclusion have built up over a long period – it will take a long time to put this right.

We have made a sound start – investing more to improve the health service, to drive up standards in education, targeting extra help on the most vulnerable in society through tax and benefit reform, and taking action to tackle problems such as teenage pregnancies. We have put particular emphasis on investing in education and on increasing opportunities, recognising that these are the best ways to achieve a lasting impact on poverty.

The right policies are the policies that work. We will continue to listen to people on the ground, including people who are themselves living in poverty, to make sure our policies are having the right effect.

We are prepared to be judged on results. In this, our first Annual Report on tackling Poverty and Social Exclusion, we set out a range of indicators against which we chart our progress.

We are proud of what we have achieved so far, but we also know there is a long way to go. Our goals are ambitious. But with determination, and a willingness to work together, we can make the vision of a fairer Britain a reality.

Alistair Darling
Secretary of State for Social Security

We're making a start — we're tackling the causes of poverty and improving opportunities for all

OUR GOAL

The Government believes that everyone should have the opportunity to achieve their potential. But too many people are denied that opportunity. It is wrong and economically inefficient to waste the talents of even one single person.

Our aim is to end the injustice which holds people back and prevents them from making the most of themselves. That means making sure that all children, whatever their background and wherever they live, get a first class education, giving them the tools they will need to succeed in the adult world. And it means making sure that children can live and play in clean, safe environments, and that the community in which they live is thriving and supportive. Put simply, our goal is to end child poverty in 20 years.

The Government is committed to tackling poverty and its causes. This report sets out the scale of the problems we face, and our strategy to tackle them. We have set ourselves challenging goals, which we know cannot be easily or quickly achieved. But we have made a strong start. And we are prepared to be judged on results. We list the indicators against which we will monitor our progress at the end of this chapter.

THE CHALLENGE FACING THE GOVERNMENT

Over the past two decades, inequality and its visible impact in the UK have increased dramatically. Major economic and social changes have contributed to this process and to escalating problems in the most deprived communities. In the past, policies have often been slow to react, and unco-ordinated in the solutions they sought to offer. The result: too many people are poorer than they should be, and dependent on benefits when they need not be.

> The proportion of people living in households with relatively low incomes more than doubled between the end of the 1970s and the beginning of the 1990s.

- The proportion of people living in households with relatively low incomes more than doubled between the end of the 1970s and the beginning of the 1990s.

One in three
children live in
households
below half
average
income.

- One in three children live in households below half average income.

- Nearly one in five working-age households has no one in work.

- The poorest communities have substantially more unemployment and experience higher levels of poor housing, vandalism and crime.

Poverty and social exclusion are complex, multi-dimensional problems. The problems we face are many:

Complex,
multi-
dimensional
problems
creating a
cycle of
disadvantage.

- **Lack of opportunities to work** – work is the most important route out of low income. But the consequences of being unemployed go wider than lack of money. It can contribute to ill-health and can deny future employment opportunities.

- **Lack of opportunities to acquire education and skills** – adults without basic skills are substantially more likely to spend long periods out of work.

- **Childhood deprivation** – with its linked problems of low income, poor health, poor housing and unsafe environments.

- **Disrupted families** – the evidence shows that children in lone parent families are particularly likely to suffer the effects of persistently low household incomes. Stresses within families can lead to exclusion; in extreme cases to homelessness.

- **Barriers to older people living active, fulfilling and healthy lives** – too many older people have low incomes, lack of independence and poor health. Lack of access to good-quality services are key barriers to social inclusion.

- **Inequalities in health** – health can be affected by low income and a range of socio-economic factors, such as access to good-quality health services and shops selling good-quality food at affordable prices.

- **Poor housing** – directly diminishes people's quality of life and leads to a range of physical and mental health problems, and can cause difficulties for children trying to do homework.

The poorest
communities
have
substantially
more
unemployment
and experience
higher levels
of poor
housing,
vandalism and
crime.

- **Poor neighbourhoods** – the most deprived areas suffer from a combination of poor housing, high rates of crime, unemployment, poor health and family disruption.

- **Fear of crime** – crime and fear of crime can effectively exclude people within their own communities, especially older people.

- **Disadvantaged groups** – some people experience disadvantage or discrimination, for example on the grounds of age, ethnicity, gender or disability. This makes them particularly vulnerable to social exclusion.

These factors act together to create a cycle of disadvantage. The effects can persist throughout people's lives. Deprivation in childhood can lead to low educational achievement and on to worse outcomes in adulthood and to poverty and social exclusion in old age. And these effects can be passed between generations. The result is socially divisive and economically inefficient.

A NEW APPROACH

In the past, attempts to deal with these issues often focused on short-term, piecemeal solutions. Huge sums were spent dealing with **immediate** problems, very little on preventing problems occurring in the **future**. Our approach is radically different. We are putting in place new solutions to old problems, working together with all sectors of society and through better working throughout government. We are:

- **tackling the causes** of poverty and social exclusion, not just the symptoms;

- creating a **fairer** society in which everyone has the **opportunity** to achieve their full potential; and

- **investing** in individuals and communities to equip them to take control of their lives.

We know that poverty and social exclusion are deep-rooted problems. This means we need:

- **long-term solutions which will pass the test of time**. We are willing to test out ideas, reject what fails and build on success. Many of the projects which we describe in this report are being introduced on a pilot basis so we can check what works best;

- **flexible action geared to local needs**. The case studies in this report illustrate the imaginative approaches being taken which have made a real difference to individuals' lives across the UK; and

- **'joined-up' government**, making sure that all our different departments and programmes are **working together** to combat the multiple problems faced by individuals and communities.

PARTNERSHIP

Our strategy is not just about government action. It is based on partnership – because real progress can only be achieved by working together. Central and local government, the voluntary sector, business communities and individuals all have vital roles to play. For too long, solutions to problems have been developed at arm's length from the individuals and communities which experience them. We are breaking down organisational and institutional barriers to create imaginative approaches to problems ranging from truancy and teenage pregnancy to rough sleeping and drug and alcohol misuse.

Creating a fairer society in which everyone has the opportunity to achieve their full potential.

Long-term, flexible and joined-up solutions to tackle the problems.

Real progress can only be achieved by working together.

DEVOLUTION

Devolution will have a major impact on the future development of policies in this field. We will work closely with the devolved administrations to tackle the problems we all face. The Government looks forward to building new partnerships in tackling poverty and social exclusion with the devolved administrations, and believes that we can learn from each other as we test new approaches to similar problems.

ACTION ACROSS THE UK

In every part of the UK, we are determined to deal with the problems of social exclusion and its causes.

- The **Scottish Social Inclusion Strategy** sets out a programme of work which is being taken forward by action teams, including development of a package of indicators covering devolved areas as a basis for monitoring success.

- The policy statement **Building an Inclusive Wales** sets out plans to produce an annual report monitoring changes in the key indicators of exclusion in Wales.

- In Northern Ireland the **New Targeting Social Need** initiative aims to tackle social need and social exclusion by targeting efforts and available resources on the most disadvantaged people, groups and areas.

- The **Social Exclusion Unit** in England is tasked with improving understanding of the key characteristics of social exclusion, and the impact of government policies, promoting solutions and making recommendations for change.

MONITORING OUR PROGRESS

We are prepared to be judged by results. There is no one single measure of poverty or of social exclusion which can capture the complex problems which need to be overcome. In this report we therefore set out a broad range of success indicators against which progress will be monitored.
It will take time to bring about fundamental change. But alongside the indicators in the report are 'policy milestones' which outline key dates in our strategy.

We will continue to review and develop the indicators, making sure they remain relevant and provide the best possible information – information we need to formulate policy to ensure the most successful results possible. Scotland, Wales and the proposed devolved administration of Northern Ireland will develop their own policies and indicators in areas for which they are responsible, to reflect their countries' particular circumstances and the needs and wishes of their people.

Here we set out the approach we are taking to tackle poverty as it affects children and young people, people of working age, older people and disadvantaged communities.

CHILDREN AND YOUNG PEOPLE – BREAKING THE CYCLE OF DISADVANTAGE

The key to tackling disadvantage in the future is the eradication of child poverty. Children who grow up in disadvantaged families generally do less well at school, and are more likely to suffer unemployment, low pay and poor health in adulthood. This poverty of opportunity is then more likely to be experienced by the next generation of children. Breaking this cycle is at the heart of our strategy for tackling poverty and social exclusion. That is why the Prime Minister has made it our aim to create a fairer society, within the next two decades, in which no child lives in poverty. We need to break the cycle of deprivation, to stop it being transmitted through generations.

Our policy priorities

- Ensuring that all children get a high-quality education wherever they go to school and providing additional help to children in the crucial pre-school years.

- Combating family poverty and social exclusion through our policies to tackle worklessness, increasing financial support for families and improving the environment in which children grow up.

- Supporting vulnerable young people, especially in the difficult transition from childhood to adult life.

Children who grow up in families which have experienced financial difficulties are, on average, less likely to stay on at school, have poorer attendance records, and are up to ten percentage points more likely to have no qualifications at age 23.

5

What we are doing – our key initiatives

- **Investment in early years** – £540 million to help vulnerable children make the best possible start in life. We are doing this through a range of initiatives including Sure Start in England and Wales, and Family Centres in Scotland. These programmes will bring together early education, health services, family support and advice on nurturing to disadvantaged families with children aged under four.

- **An additional £19 billion invested in education to raise standards**.

  - Improving **literacy and numeracy** is at the heart of our drive to raise standards. We have already seen a significant improvement in literacy and numeracy test results for 11-year-olds.

  - £500 million to reduce **exclusion and truancy**. We have already seen some improvement: the number of exclusions fell by 3 per cent in the last school year.

  - **Education Action Zones** in England will bring together schools, businesses, local authorities and communities to find innovative ways of improving education in a cluster of schools.

  - **New Community Schools** is a £26 million investment in Scotland which will provide integrated support to children and families to meet their needs and address barriers to learning.

- **Extra help for families through the tax and benefits system**.

  - The **Working Families' Tax Credit** replaces Family Credit and will provide extra help to 1.5 million families from October 1999. It will generate a minimum income of £200 a week to working families with children.

  - 1.25 million people, including 800,000 children, will be lifted above half average income by measures announced in Budget 98 and Budget 99.

- **Supporting Families**.

  - Through the **National Childcare Strategy** we are investing £470 million to ensure good-quality, affordable childcare for children aged 0–14 in every neighbourhood in England.

  - We have set up a **Ministerial Group on the Family** to help develop policies which affect families with children, and to co-ordinate family policy across government departments. Our consultation document *Supporting Families* (November 1998, Home Office) sets out the key principles for putting children's interests first and supporting parents in the challenging role of bringing up children.

- ◆ We are introducing a fairer framework of **family-friendly employee rights** including new rights to parental leave and extended rights to maternity benefits, which will help parents combine family and work responsibilities.

- **Reducing teenage pregnancy** – the Social Exclusion Unit's recent report on *Teenage Pregnancy* (June 1999, Cm 4342) sets out a programme of action to halve the rate of teenage conceptions by 2010, and increase the proportion of those who are teenage parents, in education, training or employment.

- **Quality Protects** – a £375 million programme to improve the health and education of children being looked after by social services, and to improve their opportunities when leaving care.

- Improving participation and achievement in learning by **16–18-year-olds**. Implementing the strategy outlined in the Social Exclusion Unit's report *Bridging the Gap: New Opportunities for 16–18-year-olds not in education, employment or training* (July 1999, Cm 4405) through the new **ConneXions** initiative and piloting **Educational Maintenance Allowances** that will target financial support to young people from low-income families who might otherwise be excluded from learning. Together these initiatives will help all 16–18-year-olds realise the opportunities available to them.

Together these initiatives will start to target help for disadvantaged children, tackle family poverty and help children to lay the foundations for a secure and fulfilling future.

PEOPLE OF WORKING AGE – WORK FOR THOSE WHO CAN, SECURITY FOR THOSE WHO CANNOT

In order to eradicate child poverty we need to provide opportunities for their parents to work. For most people of working age, the best way to avoid poverty and social exclusion is to be in paid work. But the enormous economic and social changes of the past 50 years – the reduction in demand for unskilled labour, the changing nature of employment patterns and family structure – have left key groups in society stranded and unable to compete in the labour market.

Many people face barriers to full participation in society – some as a result of discrimination, others are more vulnerable to poverty and social exclusion because of poor health, or they are marginalised through homelessness or drug misuse. Disadvantage has been compounded through poor access to a full range of appropriate support services. Co-ordinated and imaginative action to tackle these barriers is at the heart of our strategy to reduce social exclusion.

The proportion of working-age households where no one has a job has doubled since 1979. Lone parents, older workers, people from some ethnic minorities and people with disabilities are at particular risk of being out of work.

Our policy priorities

- Building a proactive welfare system to help people into work.

- Making work pay.

- Promoting lifelong learning to ensure people have the skills and education to respond to the modern labour market.

- Supporting vulnerable groups and those most at risk of discrimination and disadvantage.

What we are doing – our key initiatives

- **Helping people into work.**

  - The new **ONE** service is being piloted in a total of twelve areas. Four started in June 1999, with plans for a further eight from November 1999, at a cost of £79.5 million. They will focus on the specific needs of people finding work. ONE will involve closer working between the Benefits Agency and the Employment Service, providing everyone with personal advice to ensure they understand the options available to them.

  - Our £5 billion New Deal programme is helping workless people to compete for jobs in the open labour market. It includes six New Deals: for young people; for long-term unemployed people aged 25 and over; for the over-50s; for the partners of unemployed people; for people with disabilities; and for lone parents.

    - over 300,000 people have joined the **New Deal for Young People**, of whom 123,000 have found jobs (91,000 have been employed for 13 weeks or more).

    - 19,000 people have found jobs through the **New Deal for Long-term Unemployed People aged 25 and over** (16,000 of them have been employed for 13 weeks or more).

    - 21,000 lone parents have found jobs through the **New Deal for Lone Parents**.

  - We are launching **Employment Zones** to improve opportunities for the long-term unemployed in the poorest areas. They will be fully implemented in April 2000. They will include Personal Job Accounts, which will help long-term unemployed people aged 25 and over in a variety of ways. This includes helping those who want to set up their own business.

  - The **New Futures Fund**, launched in May 1998, is a unique initiative in Scotland to provide intensive support and help for young people suffering from serious disadvantage in looking for work.

- **Making work pay** – the new **10p rate of income tax** from April 1999 will halve the rate of income tax for 1.8 million workers. The **National Minimum Wage** will boost the hourly wage of almost two million low-paid workers by an average 30 per cent.

- **Lifelong learning** – throughout the UK we are encouraging participation in learning for all working-age people.

- **Equality of opportunity for people with disabilities** – a new **Disability Rights Commission** will help people with a disability secure their rights under the **Disability Discrimination Act**. This will help to end discrimination for disabled people, and will provide a central source of advice and information for people with disabilities and employers.

- **Equality of opportunity for all ages** – in June 1999 we launched the *Code of Practice for Age Diversity in Employment*, together with guidance for employers on how to adopt the Code's standards for non-ageist practices. **The Active Ageing Project** is identifying the barriers to employment faced by people aged 50 and over, with a report due in autumn 1999.

- **Better health** – **£21 billion investment in the NHS** to help secure a healthier population, as well as a new public health strategy for England, published in the White Paper *Saving Lives: Our Healthier Nation* (July 1999, Cm 4386). The White Paper sets targets for saving lives in four priority areas: cancer, heart disease and stroke, accidents and mental health. *Reducing Health Inequalities: an Action Report* (July 1999, Department of Health) published alongside the White Paper, describes the range of policies in place across government to improve the health of the worst off in society and to narrow the health gap. £290 million is being invested in **Health Action Zones** to tackle health inequalities.

- In Scotland, the White Paper *Towards a Healthier Scotland* (February 1999, Cm 4269) sets a three-pronged approach based on improving life circumstances, encouraging healthy lifestyles and addressing major health problems.

- The strategic report *Well into 2000 a positive agenda for health and well-being* (Department of Health and Social Services, Northern Ireland, 1997) sets out the Government vision, priorities and specific targets for improving health and social well-being in Northern Ireland.

- *Better Health – Better Wales* (May 1998, Cm 3922) sets out a new approach for tackling the underlying causes of ill-health.

- **Drugs** – our ten-year strategy *Tackling Drugs to Build a Better Britain* (April 1998, Cm 3945) sets out a comprehensive framework for preventing and treating drug misuse, protecting communities from drug-related anti-social and criminal behaviour, and stifling the availability of drugs.

Together these initiatives will start to tackle barriers to work, help individuals to support themselves and their families through work wherever possible, and support vulnerable groups in our society.

OLDER PEOPLE – HELPING TODAY'S AND TOMORROW'S PENSIONERS

People today can expect to live longer than in the past. We need to ensure that their retirement is a time of opportunity, fulfilment, and contribution to both their family and society. But for too many people it means financial insecurity, isolation and poor access to services. Women and members of some minority groups are at particular risk. Poor health and housing, fear of crime and inadequate public services can all limit older people's independence and ability to participate in the life of their communities.

Our policy priorities

- Ensuring that more of tomorrow's pensioners can retire on a decent income.

- Tackling the problems of low income and social exclusion among today's pensioners.

- Improving opportunities for older people to live secure, fulfilling and active lives.

What we are doing – our key initiatives

- **Pension reform which gives people real opportunities to save for their retirement**. Our Green Paper *A new contract for welfare: PARTNERSHIP IN PENSIONS* (December 1998, Cm 4179) sets out our proposals for a **New Insurance Contract for Pensioners** including:

  - the new stakeholder pension schemes which offer a better deal, particularly for middle-income earners, by providing a safe, flexible low cost vehicle to save for their retirement; and

  - dramatic improvements in pensions for low earners, carers and people with disabilities, through a new State Second Pension.

- **A new Minimum Income Guarantee** paid through Income Support for today's pensioners worth at least £75 a week for a single pensioner and £116.60 for couples from April 1999. We will increase it in line with earnings in April 2000.

For both single pensioners and pensioner couples, the average income of the richest fifth increased twice as fast as the poorest fifth.

Better opportunities for today's and tomorrow's pensioners.

- Action to tackle **fuel poverty** with a fivefold increase in the Winter Fuel Payments to £100 starting in winter 1999/2000. And proposals for a new, more generous Home Energy Efficiency Scheme, which for the over-60s would increase the maximum insulation grant to £1,800. We have also cut VAT on fuel.

- **The development of a National Service Framework for Older People** is well under way. This will set national standards of care in the NHS. It will put in place strategies to support implementation and establish performance measures.

- **Improving access to key services** – free eye tests restored for all pensioners, proposals for a new care charter addressing standards across a range of care and health issues. And a £50 million investment in rural bus services.

- **Tackling crime** – an extra £1.25 billion investment over the next three years for the police, with £170 million to extend CCTV for safer streets.

- **Action to improve access to cultural and leisure services** – such as libraries, free access to museums and galleries – and to extend opportunities for voluntary work.

- **An Inter-Ministerial Group on Older People** has been set up to co-ordinate action across government to consult older people on their needs and wishes, and to ensure that issues affecting older people are addressed in a co-ordinated way.

Together these initiatives start to build a framework for a decent and fulfilling retirement for all pensioners.

COMMUNITIES

The increasing polarisation between thriving communities on the one hand, and deprived ones on the other has been one of the key problems of our society over the past 20 years. We aim to bridge the gap between the deprived and other neighbourhoods, developing flexible solutions, which cut across traditional boundaries, in partnership with local communities.

Unemployment rates are twice as high in the 44 most deprived local authority districts compared with the rest of England.

The most deprived neighbourhoods face a concentration of linked problems – high unemployment, lack of educational opportunities, poor health, poor services, inadequate housing and high crime.

Our policy priorities

- Targeting help to areas with the greatest problems so we can tackle the root causes of poverty and social exclusion.

- Integrated policies to address the special needs of deprived areas.

What we are doing – our key initiatives

Integrated local strategies to tackle neighbourhood deprivation.

- The **New Deal for Communities**, with a budget of £800 million over the next three years, aims to regenerate the most deprived areas through improving job prospects, reducing crime, improving educational achievement and reducing poor health. The initiative will be piloted in 17 of England's poorest areas, as a test-bed for the principles of a national strategy for regeneration.

- The Social Exclusion Unit is developing a comprehensive **national strategy for neighbourhood renewal** to tackle the problems of the most deprived neighbourhoods in England. This will be published in spring 2000 for consultation.

- The Social Exclusion Unit has set up **18 Policy Action Teams** addressing a range of problems which require cross-Whitehall solutions to feed into the National Strategy for Neighbourhood Renewal. These include getting people in deprived areas into jobs; intensive, localised housing management; new approaches to raising educational achievement; improving access to financial services for those in deprived neighbourhoods; and information on how to produce integrated local strategies to tackle neighbourhood deprivation.

- Over £2.4 billion is being spent over the next three years through the **Single Regeneration Budget** for regeneration schemes run by local partnerships tackling the most deprived areas in England.

- **Health Action, Education Action and Employment Zones** have already started tackling the specific problems faced by deprived areas. The Urban and Rural White Papers will contain details of our plans to tackle the problems in particular areas.

- **IT Learning Centres** will provide people in deprived communities with the opportunity to acquire key skills needed for a modern labour market.

- £5 billion is being invested in **housing** over the lifetime of the Parliament through the release of council house capital receipts.

- In Scotland, **Social Inclusion Partnerships** are encouraging joint working to tackle social exclusion in some of the most deprived communities. £278 million of public money is being made available over the next three years for the **New Housing Partnerships** initiative. This money will lever significant resources from the private sector. Together, this will promote community ownership of housing, and improve the fabric of social housing.

- The **Capital Challenge Fund** in Wales provides support for local regeneration strategies such as the North Wales Slate Valleys initiative. The challenge is to reverse migration by creating an environment in which small enterprises and community businesses can flourish.

- We are forming **new partnerships** inside and outside government, across all sectors – we are working with other public, voluntary and private sector bodies as we all have a part to play in promoting social inclusion.

Together these initiatives are starting to identify and tackle the deep-rooted issues which must be addressed if we are to make a reality of our goal to narrow the gap between the most deprived and thriving communities.

INDICATORS OF SUCCESS

Our solutions are cross-governmental to the problems of poverty and social exclusion. We therefore need to monitor our progress by using cross-government indicators that focus on the particular problems faced by different age groups and communities.

We are determined to make a difference and we are prepared to be judged on our results. The following boxes outline the indicators and the policy milestones showing key dates in our strategy.

Ensuring that all children get a high-quality education wherever they go to school and providing additional help to children in the crucial pre-school years

Future policy milestones

- At least 250 local Sure Start programmes in England by 2001/02 and 100 per cent of families in contact with the local Sure Start programmes within the first two months of the birth of the child.

- To expand early years education provision for three-year-olds across the UK.

- Continued roll-out of Education Action Zones.

- Maths Year 2000.

Indicators of success

- An increase in the proportion of seven-year-old Sure Start children achieving level 1 or above in the Key Stage 1 English and maths tests.

- Health outcomes in Sure Start areas:
    - ◆ a reduction in the proportion of low birth-weight babies in Sure Start areas; and
    - ◆ a reduction in the rate of hospital admissions as a result of serious injury in Sure Start areas.

- An increase in the proportion of those aged 11 achieving level 4 or above in the Key Stage 2 tests for literacy and numeracy.

- A reduction in the proportion of truancies and exclusions from school.

- An increase in the proportion of 19-year-olds with at least a level 2 qualification or equivalent.

Combating family poverty and social exclusion through our policies to tackle worklessness, increasing financial support for families and improving the environment in which children grow up

Future policy milestones

- Working Families' Tax Credit replaces Family Credit – **October 1999**.

- Children's Tax Credit – **April 2001**.

continued on next page

Indicators of success

- A reduction in the proportion of children living in workless households, for households of a given size, over the economic cycle.*

- A reduction in the proportion of children in households with relatively low incomes.*

- A reduction in the proportion of children in households with low incomes in an absolute sense.*

- A reduction in the proportion of children in households with persistently low incomes.*

- A reduction in the proportion of children living in poor housing.

- A reduction in the proportion of households with children experiencing fuel poverty.

- A reduction in the rate at which children are admitted to hospital as a result of an unintentional injury resulting in a hospital stay of longer than three days.

Supporting vulnerable young people, especially in the difficult transition from childhood to adult life

Future policy milestones

- Further Education Maintenance Allowance pilots in **September 2000**.

- Youth Support Service – national arrangements from **autumn 2000**, with local services in place from **April 2001**.

- Introduce teenage pregnancy recommendations:

  - new guidance on sex education will be issued by the Department for Education and Employment for consultation by **summer 2000**;

  - guidance on criteria for the provision of effective and responsible youth contraception and advice services will be issued by the Department of Health by **summer 2000**; and

  - pilot of a new programme of co-ordinated support for pregnant teenagers and teenage parents aged under 18, in 20 areas for three years from **April 2000**.

Indicators of success

- A reduction in the proportion of 16–18-year-olds not in education or training.

- An improvement in the educational attainment of children looked after by local authorities.

- Teenage pregnancy:

  - a reduction in the rate of conceptions for those aged under 18; and

  - an increase in the proportion of those who are teenage parents, in education, employment or training.

Note: *shows indicators for the United Kingdom. All other indicators fall into devolved areas of responsibility. Devolution will allow countries to develop indicators and policies to reflect their particular circumstances and institutions.

Building a proactive welfare system to help people into work

Future policy milestones

- Pilots to help people on Incapacity Benefit into work (the £15 disregard and work trials) – **next steps to be announced in autumn 1999**.

- New Deals rolled out nationally. New Deal for the Over-50s will have Pathfinders in place from October 1999, **with national roll-out early in 2000**.

- Employment Zones will be fully implemented in **April 2000**.

- Evaluation of Code of Practice for Age Diversity in Employment – **2001**.

Indicators of success

- An increase in the proportion of working-age people in employment, over the economic cycle.*

- A reduction in the proportion of working-age people living in workless households, for households of a given size, over the economic cycle.*

- A reduction in the number of working-age people living in families claiming Income Support or income-based Jobseeker's Allowance who have been claiming these benefits for long periods of time.*

- An increase in the employment rates of disadvantaged groups – people with disabilities, lone parents, ethnic minorities and the over-50s – and a reduction in the difference between their employment rates and the overall rate.*

Making work pay

Future policy milestone

- Introduction of Working Families' Tax Credit and Disabled Person's Tax Credit – **due October 1999**.

Indicators of success

- A reduction in the proportion of working-age people with relatively low incomes.*

- A reduction in the proportion of working-age people with low incomes in an absolute sense.*

- A reduction in the proportion of working-age people with persistently low incomes.*

continued on next page

Promoting lifelong learning to ensure people have the skills and education to respond to the modern labour market

Future policy milestones

- Establish University for Industry by **2000**.

- Individual Learning Accounts: establish a national system by **2000**.

- Expand further and higher education to provide for an extra 800,000 people by **2002**.

- Develop a national strategy, following the Moser Report on improving literacy and numeracy, to reduce numbers of adults with poor basic skills.

Indicator of success

- An increase in the proportion of working-age people with a qualification.

Supporting vulnerable groups and those most at risk of discrimination and disadvantage

Future policy milestone

- Implementation of the Disability Income Guarantee – **April 2001.**

Indicators of success

- A reduction in the number of people sleeping rough.
- A reduction in cocaine and heroin use by young people.*
- A reduction in adult smoking rates in all social classes.
- A reduction in the death rate from suicide and undetermined injury.

Note: *shows indicators for the United Kingdom. All other indicators fall into devolved areas of responsibility. Devolution will allow countries to develop indicators and policies to reflect their particular circumstances and institutions.

Ensuring that more of tomorrow's pensioners can retire on a decent income

Future policy milestones

- Passage of Welfare Reform and Pensions Bill – **Royal Assent due later this year**.

- Implementation of stakeholder pension schemes – **April 2001**.

- Implementation of State Second Pension – **earliest date, April 2002**.

- Start of new annual pension statements – **2002**.

Indicators of success

- An increase in the proportion of working-age people contributing to a non-state pension.*

- An increase in the amount contributed to non-state pensions.*

- An increase in the proportion of working-age people who have contributed to a non-state pension in at least three years out of the last four.*

Tackling the problems of low income and social exclusion among today's pensioners

Future policy milestones

- Uprate Minimum Income Guarantee by earnings – **April 2000**.

- Bring forward proposals for changes to the treatment of resources (income and capital) for those receiving the Minimum Income Guarantee – **by the end of this Parliament**.

Indicators of success

- A reduction in the proportion of older people with relatively low incomes.*

- A reduction in the proportion of older people with low incomes in an absolute sense.*

- A reduction in the proportion of older people with persistently low incomes.*

- A reduction in the proportion of elderly households experiencing fuel poverty.

continued on next page

Improving opportunities for older people to live secure, fulfilling and active lives

Future policy milestones

- Introduce a National Service Framework, focusing on those parts of the health service particularly important for older people, for publication in **spring 2000**.

- The long-term care charter *You and Your Services*, outlining the services older people can expect from health and social services authorities, will be published in **April 2000**.

- Introducing free admission to museums and galleries for pensioners – **April 2000**.

Indicators of success

- A reduction in the proportion of older people whose lives are affected by fear of crime.

- An increase in healthy life expectancy at the age of 65.

- A reduction in the proportion of households containing at least one person aged 75 or over living in poor housing.

- An increase in the proportion of older people being helped to live independently.

Note: *shows indicators for the United Kingdom. All other indicators fall into devolved areas of responsibility. Devolution will allow countries to develop indicators and policies to reflect their particular circumstances and institutions.

Our goal is to bridge the gap between deprived communities and the rest

Future policy milestones

- New Deal for Communities roll-out.

- Publish Urban and Rural White Papers.

- Publication of a National Strategy for Neighbourhood Renewal by **spring 2000**.

- Launching the Community Legal Service in **2000**.

Indicators of success

These will reflect improved outcomes in four areas: long-term unemployment and worklessness; crime; health; and educational attainment.

- There is considerable work under way to develop indicators to monitor our progress in bridging the gap. This is being taken forward in the Social Exclusion Unit's Policy Action Team on Better Information; the Department of the Environment, Transport and the Regions' review of the Index of Local Deprivation; and in related work in Scotland, Wales and Northern Ireland. We will report on progress in next year's annual report.

2 The Government's Strategy

Tackling poverty of opportunity wherever it occurs

We are committed to tackling poverty, promoting social inclusion and increasing opportunity for all. We are determined to create a United Kingdom where everyone has opportunities to work, to learn, to make a contribution and to achieve their full potential. We are aiming for a society where everyone is able to enjoy the benefits of economic prosperity and to participate in community life. Our goal is for a fairer society; one where no child lives in poverty.

Poverty and social exclusion are complex problems and affect many aspects of people's lives through low incomes, lack of work, low levels of skills, lack of access to good-quality public services and lack of opportunities to live active and fulfilling lives. These deep-rooted problems have built up over a long period and tend to reinforce each other. Overcoming them will not be easy, but we have made a strong start. This report outlines our strategy for tackling poverty and social exclusion, and the policies and initiatives we have in place to do so.

> Promoting social inclusion and increasing opportunity for all.

Our strategy involves tackling the causes as well as dealing with the symptoms; we are addressing poverty of opportunity at whatever age it occurs. In order to tackle the problems faced by those of working age we need to combat disadvantage and lack of opportunity in childhood; to prevent poverty and social exclusion for older people we need to tackle the labour market barriers faced by those of working age. And for those who cannot work, we need to provide security and opportunities to lead active and fulfilling lives. The key to our strategy is providing opportunity for all.

KEY FEATURES OF POVERTY AND SOCIAL EXCLUSION TODAY

9. Poverty and social exclusion have many facets. The key features are listed below.

- **Lack of opportunities to work.** This is one of the most profound and problematic causes of poverty and social exclusion for men and women of working age and inevitably their children. Nearly one in five working-age households has no one in employment[4]; those living in these households are particularly likely to have low incomes. Two out of three non-pensioners in households with low incomes have no one in work[5]. Work is the most important route out of low income[6]. The consequences are wider than lack of money: unemployment can have a direct impact on health[7]; lack of the informal networks that come from being in work can deprive individuals of contacts that can lead to new employment and training opportunities[8]; long spells out of work can lead to a loss of skills and motivation, making it more difficult to find work in the future.

- **Lack of opportunities to acquire education and skills.** In the modern labour market, skills and qualifications are increasingly important – without skills or the opportunity to update them, the task of finding and remaining in employment is becoming more and more difficult. In particular, low levels of literacy and numeracy lead to labour market disadvantage, low pay and low incomes. Only one in eight jobs requires no numeracy skills[9]. Six in ten of those with persistently low incomes have no educational qualifications[10]. Adults with poor basic skills are substantially more likely to spend long periods out of work, and twice as likely to be made redundant or sacked from their first job, than those with good basic skills[11]. Staying on at school beyond the age of 16 leads to a significant increase in earnings potential[12].

- **Childhood deprivation.** The proportion of children who live in households with relatively low incomes has risen threefold since 1979. One in four children lives in families with persistently low incomes[13], and too many suffer from the linked problems of poor health, poor housing and unsafe environments. Too often, deprivation affects children's long-term prospects. Children born in 1958 with parents who reported financial difficulties or had children receiving free school meals were two-and-a-half times as likely to have no qualifications by the age of 33 as the rest of the population[14]. Children from low-income families have lower expectations about their future[15].

- **Disrupted families.** The evidence shows that children in lone parent families are particularly likely to suffer the effects of persistently low incomes. The absence of a second adult in the household puts greater responsibility and pressure on the parent who remains and increases their susceptibility to poverty and social exclusion. And stresses within families can lead to exclusion; in extreme cases to homelessness.

- **Barriers to older people living active, fulfilling and healthy lives.** Older people are still over-represented among those with low incomes, though less so than in the past. Single pensioners (mostly women) are particularly likely to have persistently low incomes. Low income in retirement is related to poor work histories – spells out of work and in low-paid employment are likely to reduce provision for retirement. Poor health, lack of independence, poor provision of cultural and leisure facilities, and lack of access to good-quality services also restrict older people's opportunity to live active and fulfilling lives.

- **Inequalities in health.** Poor health can exclude people from opportunities to participate in society; and poverty and social exclusion can contribute to poor health. Sir Donald Acheson's report *Inequalities in Health* outlines how people's health is affected by their incomes, a range of socio-economic factors including where they live and by their access to good-quality health services as well as access to shops selling good-quality food at affordable prices. 6 per cent of babies born to mothers from the most affluent areas of Scotland were of low birth weight, compared with 11 per cent in the most deprived areas[16]. And life expectancy at birth for a baby boy is about five years less for the two lowest socio-economic classes than the two highest[17].

- **Poor housing.** Poor housing directly diminishes people's quality of life and also leads to a range of linked problems, including poor health and can affect children's ability to do their homework. In particular, poor mental health is associated with poor housing and mental illness is a frequent cause of homelessness, whether through family breakdown or loss of independent housing. Low-income households are particularly likely to live in poor housing. Most housing is of good quality but a significant proportion of housing stock is unsatisfactory: for example, in England just over 7 per cent fails the current fitness standard[18] and in Scotland, 25 per cent of the stock suffers from problems of damp and condensation[19].

- **Poor neighbourhoods.** Living standards in most neighbourhoods have risen, but the poorest neighbourhoods have tended to become more run down, more prone to crime and more cut off from the labour market. For example, compared with the rest of England, the poorest 44 local authority districts in England have[20]:

  ♦ unemployment rates that are twice as high;

  ♦ mortality rates 30 per cent higher (adjusting for age and sex);

  ♦ almost one-and-a-half times the proportion of lone parent households

  ♦ two to three times the levels of poor housing; and

  ♦ particular problems of vandalism and dereliction.

> People's health is affected by their incomes, a range of socio-economic factors, including where they live and by their access to good-quality health services.

The poorest
284 wards in
England and
Wales in 1991
had nearly
half of their
working-age
population not
in work,
training or
education,
compared with
a quarter for
England and
Wales as a
whole.

Particular
ethnic
minorities are
hugely over-
represented
among those
with low
incomes.

And at local (ward) level the concentrations of deprivation are even worse. The poorest 284 wards in England and Wales in 1991 had nearly half of their working-age population not in work, training or education, compared with a quarter of the population in England and Wales as a whole[21]. These poorer areas have worse access to services such as shops and banks and pay more for insurance[22]. Social exclusion also occurs in rural areas due to poor access to services and isolation.

- **Fear of crime.** Crime and fear of crime can effectively exclude people in their own communities. Older people in particular may be afraid to go out on their own, or after dark. Young people can be susceptible to drug dealers and violence may be a feature of everyday life. Crime tends to be concentrated in the poorer areas. In England one estimate suggests that as much as 40 per cent of crime might occur in just 10 per cent of areas[23]. Evidence suggests that drug use is significantly higher in poor areas than in many other areas[24]. 12 per cent of people living in inner cities say the quality of their life is greatly affected by fear of crime, compared with 8 per cent overall[25].

- **Disadvantaged groups.** Britain is a multi-racial society, but **people from some ethnic minorities** are more likely to experience disadvantage. Seven out of ten households with a Pakistani or Bangladeshi head were in the poorest fifth of the income distribution in 1996/97 and this was also true for three out of ten households with a Black or Indian head[26]. **Women** are particularly likely to live on low incomes at key stages of their life cycle: both lone mothers and single women pensioners are more likely to have persistently low incomes. **People with disabilities** are around six times more likely than those without a disability to be out of work and claiming benefits. Their chance of being in employment is only about half that of the general population[27]. They are also more likely to experience greater problems with accessing goods, services and facilities.

10.   The above key features are linked in two important ways.

- **Lifelong effects.** The determinants of poverty and social exclusion at each stage of an individual's life are often found in their history. Deprivation in childhood can lead to low educational achievement and on to worse outcomes in adulthood. Long periods out of work can lead to poverty and exclusion in old age.

- **Reinforcement.** Unemployment can lead to poor health, which leads to social exclusion and problems returning to work. Poor housing can lead to worse health. Young people can get trapped in a 'no-home no-job' cycle. Deprived areas can slide into cycles of decline; people who can move out do so, leading to fewer resources in the local economy, empty houses, lack of local job networks – all factors which lead to further decline. The area becomes stigmatised and fewer people choose to live there.

HOW DID WE GET IN THIS POSITION? PAST TRENDS IN POVERTY AND SOCIAL EXCLUSION IN THE UK

The benefits of economic growth have not been shared by all ...

11. To understand fully the severity of the problem we are facing we need to consider the past. The past 20 years saw a significant increase in the numbers of people with relatively low incomes. Chart 2.1 shows the proportion of people living in households with relatively low incomes (proportion below 40, 50 and 60 per cent of mean income) more than doubled between the end of the 1970s and the beginning of the 1990s. This increase followed a period in the 1960s and 1970s during which the proportion of people with relatively low incomes remained broadly constant. The proportion of people with low incomes in absolute terms (numbers below a fixed income level) has remained roughly constant since 1979 despite average income growth of over 40 per cent[28].

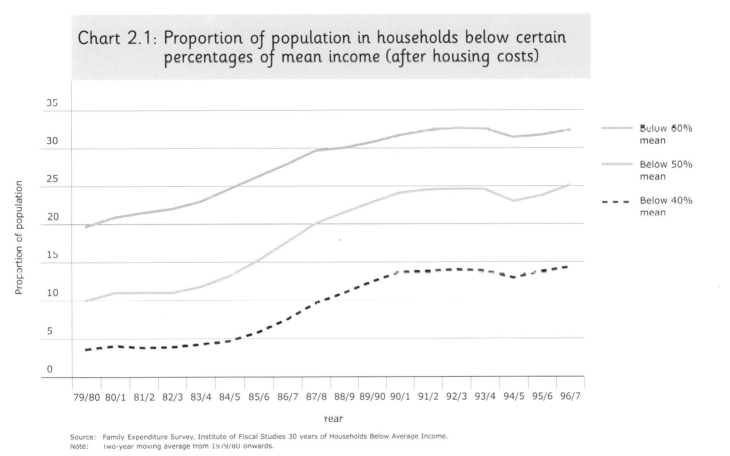

Chart 2.1: Proportion of population in households below certain percentages of mean income (after housing costs)

Source: Family Expenditure Survey, Institute of Fiscal Studies 30 years of Households Below Average Income.
Note: Two-year moving average from 1979/80 onwards.

Economic and social changes have had an impact ...

12. One of the main reasons for this increase in numbers of people with low incomes has been **the growth of numbers of working-age households where no one is working**. The proportion of working-age households where no one is working has doubled since the end of the 1970s. The proportion of workless working-age households peaked in 1996 at 18.9 per cent; by spring 1998 the proportion had declined to 17.7 per cent[29]. The growth in workless households has been driven both by a decline in male employment rates and also by an increase in the number

of single adult, including lone parent, households. In addition, employed people have become concentrated in fewer households; the rise in women's employment has occurred largely in households where their partner is already in work.

13. The most disturbing aspect of this growth in worklessness is the **number of people trapped on benefits for long periods of time**. Just under three million working-age people have been claiming income replacement benefits for more than two years[30]. Most people enter unemployment only briefly, but a significant proportion of the labour force risks repeated or prolonged periods of unemployment, which contributes to a significant detachment from work. Those who suffer a spell of unemployment tend to move into lower-waged jobs. This leads to some people being caught in a 'no-pay low-pay' cycle, with repeated spells of unemployment separated by periods of poorly-paid work[31].

14. The rewards for **investing in additional years of education** and new skills have increased dramatically. Changes in the economy over the past 30 to 40 years have transformed the nature of employment. Technological change and changes in the patterns of world trade have led to an increase in the earnings and employment rates of those with skills, relative to those without. As a result the distribution of earnings widened considerably contributing to the overall increase in income inequality. In the late 1970s, staying on at school beyond the age of 16 was associated with 40 per cent higher earnings but this rose to 60 per cent in the early 1990s. The earnings of professional and managerial workers rose relative to semi-skilled and unskilled workers[32]. Failure to acquire skills increasingly led to labour market disadvantage.

15. **Family structures** have changed dramatically and family disruption occurs more frequently. The proportion of all families who were lone parents with dependent children in the home rose from 8 per cent in 1971 to 21 per cent in 1996[33]. Compared to women with a partner in work, lone mothers became less likely to work over this period and, together with the lack of reliable support from non-resident parents, this means that lone parents and their children are highly likely to have low incomes.

16. **Older people's** average incomes after retirement have risen by more than the population as a whole. This was fuelled by increased occupational and investment income. However, the rises in incomes were greatest for those with the highest incomes.

17. On average, the **position of women** in the labour market has improved relative to men's. More women are in employment than ever before. However, while most women's life chances have improved, women are still likely to have lower incomes than men. Lone mothers and female single pensioners are particularly more likely to be trapped on low incomes. Barriers to opportunity for women – the lack of affordable, quality childcare, long periods out of the labour force while caring for dependants and the impact this has on skills – still trap women in disadvantage.

18. Major economic and social changes have contributed to the **worsening position of the poorest neighbourhoods**. The decline in traditional industries – shipbuilding, coal and steel – has affected some areas especially hard. And some of the most deprived neighbourhoods are now located in pockets within otherwise thriving areas.

... and previous policies have contributed

19. Macro-economic policies have contributed to **the cycles of boom and bust** in the past when large sections of the population lost work during the bust, but were not given enough help to get back into work during the boom. By damaging growth, high and variable inflation tends to lead to lower incomes on average.

20. **The education system** failed to keep up and adapt to the changing labour market. It failed to give **all** our children the skills they need for later life. In 1996, over 40 per cent of 11-year-olds in England failed to reach the expected standards in English and maths[34].

21. **The benefits system** has failed to adapt to changes in the labour market and society. It has become part of the problem; not the solution. As the numbers of working-age people who required support from the state in order to get by increased, the system increasingly concentrated solely on paying benefits to people, rather than providing them with active help to get off benefits. The system failed to respond to the increased numbers of lone parents and sick and disabled claimants in receipt of out-of-work benefits by providing them with new opportunities to improve their lives.

22. **The NHS**, together with better nutrition, rising incomes and better housing, has led to vastly improved health for the majority. But the improvements have not been shared equally. People who live in poor neighbourhoods tend to be ill more often and die earlier. In part, these inequalities reflect the impact of unemployment, poor housing and low income. There is some evidence that, in the past, these problems have been compounded by variations in the quality and accessibility of health services between areas.

23. **Poor housing design** can compound the problems of some areas or estates: certain design features can contribute to the prevalence of crime and feelings of isolation, making neighbourhoods less popular and unsafe. Long-term policies on housing investment, allocation, rents and benefits have tended to concentrate workless and low-income households in particular neighbourhoods.

24. **Parachuting solutions into the poorest neighbourhoods from outside** has not always worked. Some policy responses – though often well-meaning – have failed because they did not take into account the realities of people's lives[35]. Effective policy responses need to engage local people and communities.

Some of the most deprived neighbourhoods are now located in pockets within otherwise thriving areas.

Long-term policies on housing investment, allocation, rents and benefits have tended to concentrate workless and low-income households in particular neighbourhoods.

HOW WE COMPARE WITH OTHER COUNTRIES

25. The rise in income inequality experienced in the UK over the past 20 years was virtually unparalleled among OECD countries. And the UK has fared relatively badly in terms of other aspects of poverty and social exclusion as well.

   * Nearly one in five households with children has no working adult, significantly higher than all other European countries (19.5 per cent UK, 8.8 per cent France, 8.6 per cent Germany, 7.6 per cent Italy)[36].

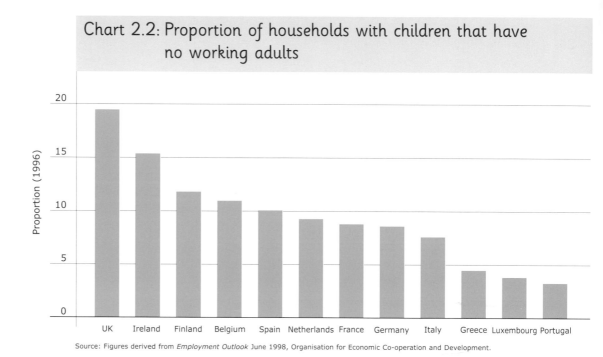

Chart 2.2: Proportion of households with children that have no working adults

Source: Figures derived from *Employment Outlook* June 1998, Organisation for Economic Co-operation and Development.

   * Teenage birth rates fell during the 1970s, 1980s and 1990s in other European countries but the UK rates have remained constant at the early 1980s level or above[37].

   * We have a lower rate of participation in education and a sharper decline in this rate between the ages of 16 and 18 than many other European countries[38].

26. We have to address these problems if we are able to compete in a world economy where knowledge-based skills are increasingly at a premium.

AIMS OF THE STRATEGY TO TACKLE POVERTY AND SOCIAL EXCLUSION

27. Our strategy is based on the principle that everybody has the right to participate in society, and the opportunity to reach their full potential. We have a threefold strategy to achieve this.

• Tackling the causes of poverty and social exclusion, not just the symptoms

28. Our aim is to prevent poverty and social exclusion occurring and recurring as well as alleviating the symptoms. Our approach of work for those who can aims to tackle the most important cause of poverty and social exclusion: being out of work. It is more effective and sustainable to help those who are out of a job back into work, where they can contribute to the well-being of society, rather than depend on state benefits. We aim to provide a sound macro-economic environment where enterprise, fairness and employment can flourish; to make work pay so that people have incentives to return to work; and to improve people's skills and their employability.

29. We aim to tackle worklessness with integrated policies that help those who have been trapped outside the labour market. Our approach is to provide help for all – including lone parents, people with disabilities, those aged over 50 and ethnic minorities – while recognising and addressing the specific and difficult barriers to work that they face.

30. Our approach is to provide security for those for whom work is not always an option. We are providing additional help through the tax and benefits system to families with children, people with disabilities and pensioners. We have provided those families with children on low incomes with a significant increase in resources. We are providing low-income pensioners with a Minimum Income Guarantee paid through Income Support. We will increase it in line with earnings in April 2000.

• Creating a fairer society in which everyone has the opportunity to achieve their full potential

31. Not only is there a sound case based on the foundations of social justice but there are also economic benefits from increasing opportunity. Economic growth depends on the extent to which everyone's talents can be fully utilised. We are putting in place policies that give people, especially those from socially excluded families and communities, the chance to reach their full potential. We are implementing policies that give greater choice and opportunity and raise the expectations of those growing up in deprived areas and families. Poor schooling, poor housing, inadequate health facilities, discrimination in all its forms, lack of skills, and aspects of the benefits system that trap people into dependence are all factors that reduce opportunity. These are all areas where we are committed to making a difference.

Giving choice and opportunity and raising the expectations of those growing up in deprived areas.

32. We aim to increase opportunities at all points in people's lives, irrespective of gender, age, disability or ethnic origin. We want to improve opportunities for children before they go to school, when they are at school and when they move from education to employment. We want to increase opportunities for employment and lifelong learning at all stages of people's working lives – when they are young, when they have children and when they approach retirement age. We want to ensure that older people can live active, fulfilling and secure lives in retirement.

Strengthening
community
life by
regenerating
deprived
communities
and involving
new partners.

- ## Investing in individuals and communities to equip them to take control of their lives

33.   The benefits of policies to tackle the causes of poverty and social exclusion will be sustainable only if they enable individuals and communities to take control of their own situations. We want to strengthen community life by regenerating deprived communities and involving new partners. Our aim is to get away from the 'single-policy', 'top-down' approach and to deliver policies in a way which is relevant to people's lives. Through local partnerships and through our consultation arrangements, we are actively engaging local people in the development and delivery of policies. We are breaking down organisational and institutional barriers to create imaginative joined-up approaches to problems including truancy, teenage pregnancy, rough sleeping and drug and alcohol misuse.

Devolution

Each country
will decide
how to
proceed in
the light of
their
particular
circumstances,
the needs
and wishes of
their people.

34.   Devolution will have a major impact on the future development of policies in this field and it is a key route by which the development of policy can be brought closer to the people. In Scotland and Wales, where matters are devolved, and the proposed future devolved administration of Northern Ireland, each country will decide how to proceed in the light of their particular circumstances, the needs and wishes of their people. The Government looks forward to building new partnerships with the devolved administrations in tackling poverty and social exclusion. The problems we face are not contained within countries. We need to work together to develop integrated policies to reduce poverty and social exclusion across the UK. And we can learn from each other as we test new approaches to similar problems.

Action across the UK

35.   Throughout the report we refer to work carried out by the Social Exclusion Unit in England, the Scottish Social Inclusion Strategy, Building an Inclusive Wales and Targeting Social Need in Northern Ireland. Boxes 2.1–2.4 (opposite) provide some background on each of these country-based strategies.

Box 2.1: Scotland – the Scottish Inclusion Strategy

In March 1999, the **Scottish Social Inclusion Strategy** set out a programme of work to develop new ideas for action and support best practice in key areas of Social Inclusion Policy. Action underway includes the preparation of:

- a report on **excluded young people**;
- a report on **inclusive communities**;
- a report on **the impact of local anti-poverty action**;
- an **evaluation framework**; and
- a report on **making it happen**.

Action teams covering these areas will report in the autumn of 1999.

A Ministerial Poverty and Inclusion Task Force has been established under the chairmanship of the Minister for Communities – its remit is to promote the development and implementation of effective, integrated policies and programmes to promote social inclusion in Scotland.

The Scottish Executive is committed to publishing its Social Inclusion Strategy this year.

Box 2.2: Wales – Building an Inclusive Wales

The policy statement *Building an Inclusive Wales* (March 1999, the Welsh Office) sets out the priorities for improving the response at all levels of government, working in partnership, to tackling the problems of social exclusion, including an annual monitoring report. It identifies four key priorities for action:

- **an annual report** monitoring changes in the key indicators of social exclusion in Wales and appraising progress across the Assembly;
- strengthening the **Social Exclusion Network**, charging it with reviewing key policy areas;
- building on the **'People in Communities'** use of 'social exclusion champions', adapting the approach to other key areas such as health groups;
- promoting **effective joint working** by streamlining planning requirements across a range of services, giving more freedom on how delivery is carried out but monitoring results more closely.

The objectives of *Building an Inclusive Wales* will be achieved through mainstream programmes, supplemented by a new Social Inclusion Fund totalling £48 million over three years, to support a range of initiatives in Wales.

Box 2.3: Northern Ireland – New Targeting Social Need

The White Paper *Partnership for Equality* (March 1998, Cm 3890) sets out the Government's plans for a **New Targeting Social Need (New TSN)** initiative to tackle social need and social exclusion in Northern Ireland. New TSN has a particular focus on combating the problems of unemployment and on increasing employability. It is also concerned with reducing need and inequalities in health, education and housing. It includes **Promoting Social Inclusion (PSI)** which involves departments working together and with interests outside government to identify and tackle causes of social exclusion which cut across departmental boundaries. PSI will tackle a series of issues, concentrating on a small number at any one time.

The first priority areas to be tackled under PSI are:

- a strategic approach to the needs of **ethnic minority groups**;
- action to alleviate the needs of **travellers**;
- the problems of **teenage parenthood**; and
- strategies for making services more accessible to **minority groups and others at risk of exclusion**.

The Northern Ireland Office and every Northern Ireland Department are preparing draft Action Plans showing how they will implement New TSN over the next three years.

Box 2.4: England – the Social Exclusion Unit

The Social Exclusion Unit (SEU) was set up by the Prime Minister in December 1997. Its remit is to help improve government action to reduce social exclusion by producing 'joined-up solutions to joined-up problems'. Most of its work is on specific projects, such as teenage pregnancy, which the Prime Minister chooses following consultation with other Ministers and suggestions from interested groups. Among the projects the SEU has undertaken are:

- **neighbourhood renewal**;
- **rough sleeping**;
- **teenage pregnancy**;
- **truancy and school exclusion**; and
- **16–18-year-olds not in education, employment or training**.

Action to eliminate poverty and social exclusion overseas

36. While this report focuses on the UK, we know that the problems of poverty and social exclusion prevail throughout the world, especially in developing countries where the problems can be particularly extreme. We are committed to working with the international community to reduce poverty abroad (see Box 2.5).

Box 2.5: Work to eliminate poverty and social exclusion overseas

Our strategy for eliminating world poverty is outlined in our White Paper *Eliminating World Poverty: A Challenge for the 21st Century* (November 1997, Cm 3789). As in the UK, our strategy is to tackle the structural causes of poverty and social exclusion rather than merely dealing with the symptoms. Through these efforts we seek to create a safer and more prosperous world which, in turn, helps to create the global conditions for employment creation, poverty reduction and enhanced opportunities at home as well as abroad.

We are committed to reversing the decline in aid spending so that we can concentrate additional resources on priority needs such as health, education and the provision of clean water. We cannot achieve this alone.

We are working with the international community to increase the poverty focus of multilateral institutions and to bring about greater consistency in policies affecting developing countries such as trade, investment and agriculture. We are building stronger partnerships with democratic governments who share our concerns. We have taken steps to relieve the burden of debt borne by poor countries through the Heavily Indebted Poor Countries initiative and other actions. And we will be reporting in 2000 on the agreements made at the 1995 World Summit for Social Development on the Copenhagen programme of action.

Further information on the UK Government's international poverty reducing strategy can be found in the Department for International Development's *Departmental Report 1999* (March 1999, Cm 4210).

MONITORING OUR PROGRESS

37.   We are prepared to be judged by results and we have, therefore, identified a broad range of indicators by which we can monitor our progress. Each chapter shows how the indicators are linked to the policy priorities we have defined for each age group (see **Chapter 1**). Poverty and social exclusion are complex problems. Our view is that they cannot be measured by a single indicator. Our approach has been to adopt a range of indicators capturing many of the aspects of poverty and social exclusion: income, employment, education, health, housing, and pension provision, for example. Income indicators form an important part of our range of indicators. Our approach to monitoring income is to use a range of indicators that capture our progress in raising the incomes of poorer people both in real terms and in relation to incomes of the population as a whole. By using a range of low income measures we should be able to provide a comprehensive assessment of our progress.

38.   Our policies provide solutions for the long term; many of the problems we face have grown up over generations. We have set out some strategic policy milestones to enable us to check whether we are on track in the short term in implementing policies to meet our longer-term aims.

39.   These indicators build on indicators and targets already in place. Some are related to the success measures proposed in the Green Paper *New ambitions for our country: A NEW CONTRACT FOR WELFARE* (March 1998, Cm 3805), taking into account responses we have had to consultation. A number of others relate to specific targets set in Public Service Agreements[39]. Others reflect targets and indicators developed for specific groups: for example the Social Exclusion Unit's report on teenage pregnancy set out our target for reducing the number of conceptions by girls aged 18 and under.

40.   Many of the indicators in the report will be applicable across the UK. However, there are a number of areas where responsibility for the policies that influence the indicator rests with the devolved administrations of Scotland and Wales and any future devolved administration in Northern Ireland. The end of **Chapter One** shows where the indicators relate to the UK and where responsibility falls to devolved areas. Work on developing indicators and policies, for devolved areas, is being taking forward to reflect each country's particular needs, circumstances and institutions.

   *   One of the Action Teams established under the **Scottish Social Inclusion Strategy** has been asked to identify key indicators of social exclusion. The Team has already surveyed existing indicators of social exclusion in Scotland, and developed a draft evaluation framework, as a basis for assessing the success of action to promote social inclusion. This will be the subject of further consideration as the Scottish Executive prepares its own social inclusion strategy.

- The policy statement **Building an Inclusive Wales** sets out plans to produce an annual report monitoring changes in the key indicators of exclusion in Wales and appraising progress against the Welsh Assembly's area of responsibility.

- In Northern Ireland, departments have developed Action Plans to show how they will implement **New Targeting Social Need (TSN)**; these will include any work which is required to ensure that they have the data they need to monitor progress and track change over time.

41. There is considerable work under way to develop indicators to monitor our progress in bridging the gap between deprived communities and the rest. The **Social Exclusion Unit's** Policy Action Team on better information, and further work to improve the Department of the Environment, Transport and the Regions' Local Index of Deprivation, will provide better ways of monitoring progress at community level. We will report on our progress in monitoring improvements at community level in next year's report.

3 Children and young people

Extending opportunities to all children

Our objective is to create a society, in the next two decades, in which no child lives in poverty and where all children have opportunities to realise their full potential. Improving opportunities for disadvantaged children is at the heart of our strategy. Far too many children grow up in poverty. And these children generally do less well at school, and are more likely to suffer unemployment, low pay and poor health in adulthood. In turn they pass on poverty of opportunity to their own children.

We are determined to reverse this process by:

- ensuring that all children get a high-quality education wherever they go to school and providing additional help to children in the crucial pre-school years;

- combating family poverty and social exclusion through our policies to tackle worklessness, increasing financial support for families and improving the environment in which children grow up; and

- supporting vulnerable young people, especially in the difficult transition from childhood to adult life.

We are providing parents with additional financial support to help them care for their children. We aim to provide all children with the basic education they need to do well in later life. And we are providing additional support for those who face problems when moving from childhood to adulthood. By tackling all these problems together we aim to create a 'virtuous cycle' rather than the 'vicious circle' that has previously trapped these families. These policies lay the foundations for a better future for all our children and for society as a whole.

Aiming to create a 'virtuous cycle' rather than the 'vicious circle' that traps families.

THE PROBLEM

1. Children are now more than twice as likely to live in families without a parent in work than children were a generation ago. Too many live in families with persistently low incomes and in unhealthy, unclean and unsafe environments. Some children from disadvantaged homes rise above the obstacles they experience and make a success of their lives. But we know that disadvantage in childhood can result in children being unable to develop their full potential. This leads to a poorer society for all of us.

Key features of poverty and social exclusion

2. There is a vast disparity in the quality of children's lives in the UK. No single aspect or statistic captures all the disadvantages caused by poverty and social exclusion but we can identify some key features.

- **Low income.** Children are disproportionately likely to be living in low-income households. 40 per cent of children live in the bottom 30 per cent of the income distribution[1]. One in four children live in households with persistently low incomes compared with one in five of the population as a whole[2]. The proportion of children living in households with relatively low incomes has increased dramatically: in 1995/96 one in three children lived in households with below half average income, compared with one in ten in 1979.

Box 3.1: Key features of poverty and social exclusion[3]

Certain groups of children are particularly likely to be living in households which have low incomes. Those most at risk of being in the bottom 30 per cent of the income distribution include children living:

- in larger families (those with four or more children) – 73 per cent of these are in the bottom 30 per cent of the income distribution;

- in families with young mothers, aged 16–24 – a 68 per cent chance;

- in ethnic minority families – a 65 per cent chance;

- in lone parent families where the parent has never been married – a 79 per cent chance; or divorced or separated – a 66 per cent chance;

- without a working parent – an 86 per cent chance; and

- with parent(s) without educational qualifications – a 54 per cent chance.

- **Parents who are out of work.** Nearly one in five children live in a household where no one works[4]. Chart 3.1 shows that the proportion of children living without a parent in work doubled between 1979 and 1996/97. These families make up the majority of those on low incomes. Not only does this lead to financial disadvantage but, as a result, a large proportion of children (2.7 million) are growing up in a household that depends on Income Support or income-based Jobseeker's Allowance as a source of income[5]. Over half of their parents have been on Income Support or income-based Jobseeker's Allowance for more than two years and one in three has been claiming for five years or more.

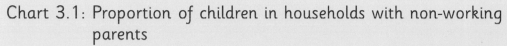

Chart 3.1: Proportion of children in households with non-working parents

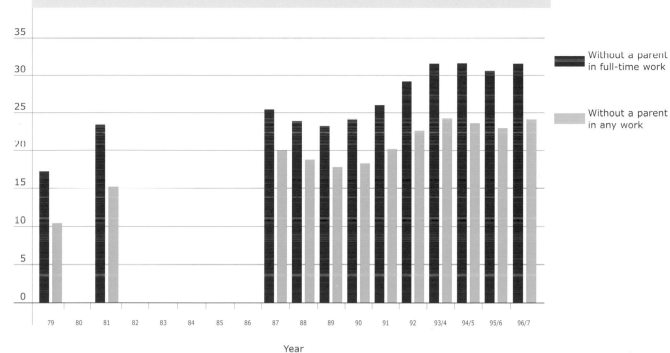

Without a parent in full-time work

Without a parent in any work

Proportion

Year

79 80 81 82 83 84 85 86 87 88 89 90 91 92 93/4 94/5 95/6 96/7

Source: Households Below Average Income (HBAI) Family Expenditure Survey.
Note: HBAI data not available for 1980 and 1982–86.

- **Access to educational opportunities.** Children from disadvantaged homes face greater barriers to achieving their potential at school. There is considerable evidence that growing up in a family which has experienced financial difficulties damages children's educational performance[6]. Children going to schools in poorer areas (where more than 35 per cent of pupils are in receipt of free school meals) tend to do less well at school – only 41 per cent of children in these schools achieved level 4 or above in the Key Stage 2 (age 11) maths test compared with 59 per cent of all children in 1998[7] (see Chart 3.2 overleaf). Children from poorer areas are more likely to play truant and be excluded from school. In secondary schools serving 'difficult to let' estates, truancy is four times the national average[8].

- **Health inequalities.** Infants and children in social classes IV and V have higher rates of infant mortality and chronic illness than those in social classes I and II. In 1993–95 the infant mortality rate for social class V was 70 per cent higher than the rate for social class I[9]. Equally, children in the lower social groups are more likely to have accidents – children up to the age of 15 from unskilled families are five times more likely to die from unintentional injury than those from professional families[10]. Children in low-income families are less likely to eat a healthy and balanced diet and are more likely to become smokers. While fruit and vegetable consumption across all income groups is less than the recommended five portions a day, there is a marked trend towards the lowest consumption being among the lower socio-economic groups[11]. Those in social classes IV and V are less likely to have given up smoking by the time they reach their 30s than those in the higher social classes[12] – with a long-term detrimental impact on their health.

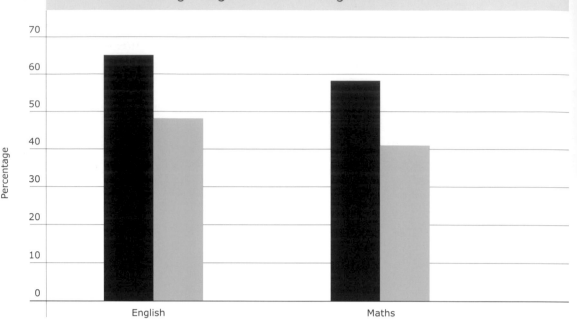

Chart 3.2: Proportion of 11-year-olds achieving level 4 or above in Key Stage 2 tests in England in 1998

Legend:
- All 11-year-olds
- 11-year-olds in schools receiving 35% or more free school meals

Source: Department for Education and Employment (DfEE).

- **Poor environments.** Around one in five households with infants where the head of the household is employed part time, is unemployed or is otherwise economically inactive live in poor housing. And over one in four unemployed lone parents with infants live in poor housing compared with 14 per cent of the population as a whole[13]. Damp, inadequate heating and overcrowding are associated with general ill-health and respiratory disorders, accidental injury and emotional problems. Adverse effects on children's health are considered to last into adult life[14]. Fire risk is greatest for those in the poorest social rented housing and in temporary accommodation[15]. And children up to the age of 15 from unskilled families are 15 times more likely to die in a fire in the home than those from professional families[16].

3. These features are linked. Children in low-income families are disproportionately more likely to suffer from poor health and live in worse environments. Children experiencing poor health tend to do less well at school. This means that to make a difference we need to tackle all the problems simultaneously: improving health and education services; ensuring children grow up in decent quality housing; and helping parents back to work.

- **Children of teenage mothers.** Infant mortality rates are highest for mothers aged under 20[17]. They also have an increased risk of poor housing and bad nutrition. Daughters of teenage mothers are more likely than the daughters of older mothers to become teenage mothers themselves[18].

- **Ethnicity.** Discrimination and language barriers add to social exclusion. Children from some ethnic minorities are significantly more likely to be excluded from school. Black Caribbean pupils are four times as likely to be excluded from school compared with the white population[19].

- **Disability.** Children with disabilities are nearly twice as likely to be living without a parent in work than children without disabilities[20]. Some children with disabilities and those with long-term physical or mental health problems may fall behind at school because of absence, or be denied access to courses of their choice. They are particularly likely to be living in low-income households.

The consequences of poverty and social exclusion for children's futures

4. Poverty and social exclusion not only have an impact on the quality of children's lives on a daily basis, they also affect their futures. A growing body of research indicates that children's life chances are affected by who their parents are, as well as by their own talents and efforts. Key findings are that:

   - poverty in childhood increases the likelihood of low income in adulthood[21];

   - there is a strong association between children's earnings and those of their parents. Only a third of boys whose fathers were in the bottom quarter of the earnings distribution made it to the top half when they grew up and the pattern is similar for girls[22]. Men whose fathers were unemployed are twice as likely to be unemployed for a year or more between the ages of 23 and 33[23]; and

   - people's chances of being in a manual occupation, having no access to a car and living in rented accommodation are also higher if their parents were in the same position[24].

5. Not all children born into low-income families fare badly in later life. The research indicates that just as there is a range of factors that increase the risk of deprivation being passed across generations, there is also a range of factors that can help break this spiral of disadvantage. An important component in our strategy is to boost the protective factors and attack the risk factors.

Children's life chances are affected by who their parents are, as well as by their own talents and efforts.

6. There are **key risk factors** occurring during childhood and adolescence which research suggests increase the likelihood that disadvantaged children will fare worse in later life.

    - **Poor early development.** The earliest years of life (even before birth) are very important in terms of child development and future health. Children with higher birth-weight and better nutrition develop better[25].

    - **Poor school attendance.** Children with poor school attendance are less likely to do well later in life. Persistent truants are four times more likely not to be in education, training or employment at age 16 than all children[26].

    - **Being 'looked after' by a local authority.** Boys who have been in foster homes or in care are more likely to be unemployed adults than those who lived with their natural parents[27].

    - **Contact with the police.** Having contact with the police when growing up is associated with significantly worse educational qualifications[28], leading on to worse outcomes in later life.

    - **Drug misuse.** Young people who become involved in drug misuse are at risk of dropping out of school and of missing out on educational and training opportunities. They are also more likely to fall into other criminal activity.

    - **Teenage parenthood.** The risk of teenage pregnancy is greatest for young people who have grown up in poverty and disadvantage or those with poor educational achievement. Further, teenage parents tend to remain poor and they are disproportionately likely to suffer relationship breakdown. Their health and their children's is worse than average[29].

    - **Non-participation in education, employment and training between the ages 16–18.** Being out of education, employment or training for more than six months between the ages 16–18 is the most powerful predictor of unemployment at age 21[30].

7. Many of these factors are linked – for example, young women in care have repeatedly been shown to be at higher risk of teenage pregnancy and teenage parents are more likely to drop out of education early[31].

8. Research also suggests that there are some important **protective factors** that can increase the likelihood that children achieve their potential.

    - **Parental interest matters.** The research suggests that parental attitudes and interest in education have a significant effect on educational attainment. Helping parents and supporting them is a key element of our strategy.

Parental interest has a significant effect on educational attainment.

- **Good schools and good teachers make a difference.** The relationship between local deprivation and school performance is not exact: some high-performing schools exist in poor areas. Children from disadvantaged backgrounds who succeed at school are significantly more likely to be upwardly mobile[32].

- **Aspirations.** Children in low-income families tend to have lower aspirations and expectations for their future. They are much more likely to want jobs which typically take a minimal amount of time to train for and, on the whole, require few, if any, academic qualifications[33]. For a young person, early parenthood may not seem such a bad option if they have grown up in poverty, have difficult family relationships and low expectations of a good job[34]. We want to tackle this poverty of ambition. We want to work with parents to involve them as partners in their children's education. We need to challenge the assumption that schools in deprived areas cannot make a difference. And we need to ensure that all children aspire to fulfil their full potential.

Encouraging new ambitions.

WHAT WE ARE DOING – OUR POLICY PRIORITIES

9. In order to achieve our goal, we are adopting a three-pronged approach to tackle the root causes of poverty and social exclusion, to give all children the best possible chance in life.

- **Ensuring that all children get a high-quality education** wherever they go to school and providing additional help to children in the crucial pre-school years.

- **Combating family poverty and social exclusion** through our policies to tackle worklessness, increasing financial support for families and improving the environment in which children grow up.

- **Supporting vulnerable young people**, especially in the difficult transition from childhood to adult life.

Ensuring that all children get a high-quality education wherever they go to school and providing additional help to children in the crucial pre-school years

Crucial early interventions to reverse the cycle of inter-generational poverty.

10. Providing every child with a decent education is essential for the prevention of future poverty. Educational attainment is the most important route into work, and out of poverty and social exclusion. That is why we are making a £19 billion investment in education over three years to tackle the problems in our schools and to equip our children to play a full part in society when they grow up.

Providing a better start for vulnerable families

11. Differences in opportunity start at birth. At the age of 22 months, children whose parents are in social classes I and II with higher education levels are already 14 percentage points higher up the educational development distribution than children whose parents are in social classes IV and V or have low educational attainment.

12. The period before a child attends school for the first time is of vital importance for long-term social inclusion. The central challenge is to ensure that every child arrives at school healthy and ready to learn. This means we need to increase opportunities and to provide effective, integrated support that addresses both the needs of children and their parents.

13. The period before and immediately after birth is crucial to a child's development and future prospects. We are addressing this through help to the poorest families.

   - The **Sure Start** strategy: in April 1999 the first 21 Sure Start programmes were announced. They will offer help to families with children from birth up to the age of four, in areas where children are most at risk from poverty and social exclusion. In Scotland, new help for families with young children is being provided through the expansion of **Family Centres** and the provision of part-time, pre-school education for children aged over three (see Box 3.3) as well as a new **Starting Well** scheme focusing on health and protection from harm for children.

   - Through the **National Childcare Strategy** we aim to ensure good-quality, affordable childcare for children aged 0–14 in every neighbourhood. £470 million will be invested in childcare in England over the lifetime of this Parliament, including £170 million from the New Opportunities Fund to support new out-of-school services. During 1998/99 we created 60,000 new childcare places and provided a free nursery school education place for every four-year-old whose parents wanted it. From September 1999 free nursery places will be extended to some 50,000 three-year-olds. In Northern Ireland the consultation on the childcare strategy **Children First** is seeking views on how policies and support for families with young children can best be further developed.

Box 3.3: Support for the early years

Sure Start will offer joined-up help from a range of service providers to families with children aged under four, in areas where they are most at risk from social exclusion.

Working with parents, Sure Start aims to promote the physical, intellectual, social and emotional development of young children to make sure they are ready to thrive when they go to school. Sure Start programmes are set in some of the most disadvantaged areas of the country and will bring together early education, health services, family support and advice on nurturing for all families with children aged under four when they need it.

Sixty areas of England have been identified as 'trailblazer' districts and have been asked to work with all local partners to develop programmes which can meet the key values and aims of Sure Start. £452 million is being invested in 250 Sure Start programmes in England. Similar programmes are being put in place elsewhere in the United Kingdom.

In Wales the focus will be in line with the common philosophy for Sure Start in England, aimed at improving health, the ability to learn and promoting social development. £3 million will be made available in year one with plans to increase it to £11 million in each of the two succeeding years.

In Scotland **Family Centres**, with extra resources of £42 million, have been expanded to support families with children aged three and under to target areas of greatest need. In addition to this, the **Starting Well** initiative will focus on health promotion and protection from harm for children from the period leading up to birth to the first five years of childhood. It is expected to incorporate, for example, encouraging and supporting parents; reducing the instances of child injury; promoting better diet and nutrition; and encouraging breastfeeding. By improving children's health in this way, we can improve their opportunities to develop and learn.

Box 3.4: Sport and recreation

Play has a major role in the Government initiatives designed to benefit children and families: Sure Start, the National Childcare Strategy, Health Action Zones, after-school clubs, New Deal for Communities, the work of the Social Exclusion Unit and the recently announced Green Spaces project. Children who play, learn to talk and work together are more likely to be healthy and active – physically, mentally and emotionally. They also do better academically.

Through our policy of **Sport for All**, we are encouraging young people to participate in sport from an early age and throughout their lives at all levels. To complement our approach, additional funding will be made available to schools through the Lottery Sports Fund.

A positive
contribution
to early
development
– a strong
foundation
for life.

Early years education

14. Our early years policies make a positive contribution to children's early development and allow them to build on this foundation throughout their lives.

- We have already ensured that since September 1998 all four-year-olds can have an early education place.

- New resources will help us meet our target of expanding early education provision for three-year-olds in England from 34 to 66 per cent by 2001/02. These places are available in the maintained, private and voluntary sectors and are being co-ordinated by 150 Early Years Development and Childcare Partnerships.

- Public libraries also have a key role in developing early years reading centres and promoting a general interest in reading among pre-school children. We are working with local authorities to improve services and standards.

Case study 3.1: Example of an Early Excellence Centre

The pilot programme of **Early Excellence Centres** provides models of good practice in integrating high-quality early years education, care, family support and other services, working with Early Years Development and Childcare Partnerships and others to help raise standards elsewhere.

One of the centres in the north-west of England was formed by a nursery school and family centre merging and unifying their structures. Supported by Department for Education and Employment funding, it is providing additional integrated all-year education and care places for local children and families. It has a positive commitment to multi-agency outreach work in the community and strong links with health professionals. On-site, adults can access a range of training, with care provision for their children when they need it.

Case study 3.2: The Hillfields Early Years Centre

The **Hillfields Early Years Centre** in Coventry is committed to developing children's confidence as the basis for early learning, working in partnership with parents to provide the best opportunities for each child – including those with special needs – and improving the employment prospects of local families. It provides integrated education, childcare and family support services and operates a programme of training and support for early years workers and foster carers. Parental support begins with home visiting and includes informal contacts for young mothers, literacy and numeracy activities, adult education and more formal further education. One mother has recently begun a degree course at Coventry University. There is accredited training for childminders and playgroup staff. Training opportunities are supported by day care provision for children aged under two. The Centre is also a base for research and development in the integrated delivery of early years services.

15. The Pre-School Education Expansion Programme in Northern Ireland has the long-term aim of providing a year of pre-school education for every child. Additional pre-school places are being targeted in the first instance on the most socially disadvantaged children and on the oldest pre-school children. £38 million will have been made available for the programme by 2001/02, and a total of 9,200 additional places secured. As a result, the proportion of children benefiting from pre-school education in their first pre-school year will be almost doubled, to 85 per cent. In Scotland a free part-time education place is now available for virtually every Scottish child in the pre-school year; and an extra £138 million has been committed over the next three years to ensure that, by 2002, pre-school places are available for all three-year-olds.

Improving literacy and numeracy

16. Acquiring basic literacy and numeracy skills is essential for all children if they are to continue to learn and succeed to their full potential. Improving literacy and numeracy in primary schools is crucial to our strategy of tackling the causes of poverty and social exclusion at source. And standards will need to rise most quickly in some of the most disadvantaged areas.

17. Ambitious national targets have been set to increase the proportion of 11-year-olds reaching the expected standard for their age to 80 per cent for literacy and 75 per cent for numeracy by 2002. We have already seen improvements. The proportion of 11-year-olds reaching level 4 or above in the Key Stage 2 tests for literacy rose by five percentage points between 1998 and 1999. And the proportion achieving level 4 or above in the Key Stage 2 tests for numeracy rose by ten percentage points between 1998 and 1999.

Raising standards of literacy and numeracy in primary schools.

18. The **National Literacy and Numeracy Strategies** were developed to help schools and Local Education Authorities (LEAs) meet these targets. The Literacy Hour, which was introduced in September 1999, is now in place in virtually all primary schools. From September 1999, primary schools will be expected to teach a daily mathematics lesson. Funding of £120 million a year for the next three years has been supplemented this year by a further £48 million to help pupils who have fallen behind. In addition, since taking office in 1997, the Government has given schools a total of £115 million to spend on books.

19. The **National Year of Reading**, which will continue under the banner of the National Reading Campaign, has celebrated the pleasures of books and encouraged parents to read with and to their children. Organisations outside the formal school environment, particularly libraries, but also cultural and sporting organisations, have also made strong contributions to the National Year of Reading. **Maths Year 2000** will similarly back teachers' efforts in the classroom by involving parents, business and the wider community and helping people of all ages to improve their skills in maths.

> ## Case study 3.3: London Leopards and the National Year of Reading
>
> The National Year of Reading began in September 1998 at the start of the academic year. As a way of interesting more children in reading, each month of the year was given a different theme. March was 'sports month' and the London Leopards basketball team was linked with 10 schools in the London Boroughs of Lewisham and Greenwich which had been identified by OFSTED as requiring special measures.
>
> A Leopard team member was allocated to each school, which he visited several times and got to know the pupils. Each school was free to decide how to use the team member in a programme of pupil-focused support in the schools to contribute to raising standards for the pupils and for the schools as a whole. The players attended school assemblies and introduced a competition to produce the best project, following on from work on a basketball book in class. As part of the project the children were invited to a basketball game between the London Leopards and the Manchester Giants, at which they were able to take part in basketball and literacy competitions.

A high-quality education from every school

20.   Providing all children with a high standard of education, irrespective of their family background and where they live, is essential if we are to tackle the poverty of opportunity at its roots. Many schools already offer this, but the picture is not consistent. We are committed to raising standards.

- Encouraging all parents to take an active role in their children's education. This means they should know what to expect from the education system – we need greater transparency and better accountability. That is why we are setting out, clearly, our targets for schools.

- **Education Development Plans.** From April 1999, each LEA in England must have a Plan in place, setting out the targets agreed with its schools and its strategies for helping schools meet them through effective partnerships.

- **Class sizes.** Throughout the UK there are targets to reduce class sizes, for the first three years of primary school, to 30 pupils or less.

- **Excellence in Cities.** We aim to raise standards in selected city areas where problems are most acute. There will be more choice for parents and more help for children to achieve their potential. 50 Education Action Zones (see next page), focusing on low performance in small clusters of schools, have been selected for Excellence in Cities.

- **IT access for all schools.** We aim to connect every school in the UK to the information superhighway by 2002, with funds from the £656 million available to set up the National Grid for Learning.

- **IT learning centres in schools.** Of the £470 million allocation from the Capital Modernisation Fund in the 1999 Budget, around £100 million will be spent on establishing learning centres within schools in city areas in England. They will offer extended opening hours and new homework facilities and ensure that children from the poorest families are not disadvantaged through a lack of quality Information and Communication Technology (ICT) facilities at home.

21. Setting standards for schools is important in ensuring all schools provide children with the best possible education. But we also need to have in place mechanisms for ensuring that all schools live up to those standards.

- **Inspection.** Office for Standards in Education (OFSTED) reports will complement the Education Development Plans. Taken together, they will provide a comprehensive system for LEAs to measure performance and consider how to improve quality and value for money.

- **Schools requiring special measures.** Schools which are failing to provide an acceptable standard of education must now be turned around within two years. The number of failing schools is now reducing for the first time since regular inspection began, and the average time spent in bringing them back up to standard has reduced from 25 to 18 months.

- **Schools with serious weaknesses.** New arrangements are now in place for schools identified as having serious weaknesses. These schools must set targets to address their problems within one year, supported by their LEA. All seriously weak schools will be inspected by OFSTED and HMI within two years.

- **Education Action Zones.** 25 Education Action Zones (EAZs) have been established around the country and a further 47 have been short-listed and are currently undertaking development work on their applications. The start date for each Zone will be agreed in discussion with applicants, ranging from September 1999 to September 2000. Each Zone receives public and private sector funding of up to £1 million a year for a period of three or five years. Zones follow a multi-agency approach, bringing together agencies such as health and social services, crime prevention, careers, and further and higher education.

  - ◆ 13 Zones have introduced some flexibility into the National Curriculum at Key Stage 4.

  - ◆ 6 Zones have businesses in the lead role and 19 are taking action to reduce exclusions and improve levels of attendance and behaviour.

  - ◆ 10 Zones have taken action to vary the length of the school day or year.

Case study 3.4: Firfield Community School

Firfield Community School (formerly known as Blakelaw School) in Newcastle was one of the first schools in the country to be given a Fresh Start. Blakelaw School went into special measures in April 1996. Under the Fresh Start initiative, the school has been given a new identity with new management, improved buildings, security and a good quality of education for all. Firfield is one of two secondary schools in Newcastle's Education Action Zone to benefit from business partners including Marks & Spencer plc and British Telecom plc. The new Firfield School opened in September 1998.

Making sure that all children benefit from increased opportunities

22. Too many of our children miss out on opportunities at school, because they play truant or are excluded, or because they need extra help but do not receive it. We are taking steps to address this.

   - **Exclusions and truancies.** £500 million is being invested over the next three years to reduce exclusion and truancy in schools and to raise the attainment levels of children at risk of social exclusion. A range of innovative projects are in place to tackle disaffection and we are investing in specific action aimed at those pupils excluded for more than 15 days. This will be of particular benefit to children from certain ethnic groups and those looked after by local authorities who are over-represented in the exclusion figures. We have already seen some improvement: the number of exclusions fell from 12,700 in 1996/97 to 12,300 in 1997/98[35].

   - We are piloting a new **Youth Support Service** from April 2000 to support schools in reducing exclusion and truancy, and making sure that young people get the help they need to make the best possible use of their educational opportunities; helping prepare young people at Key Stages 3 and 4 for post-16 options.

Case study 3.5: Springvale County Primary School, Staffordshire

This school was part of the Gladiator Challenge Pilot which aims to improve attendance and punctuality in targeted schools. Each child has a 'Gladiator Challenge' card, which shows 'The Wall' as used in the Gladiator Challenge show. For every day the child attends a sticker is placed on the card, a whole week's attendance gains a special 'G' sticker as 'another week bites the dust'. The challenge card runs for a half term, after which the child is presented with their card. The next half term starts a new challenge. Certificates for excellent attendance are presented by a Gladiator at a special Gladiator Event day.

- **Study Support.** Between 1999 and 2001, £180 million of lottery money from the New Opportunities Fund will be allocated to out-of-school-hours learning in at least half of all secondary and special schools and a quarter of all primary schools. In England this amounts to over 6,000 schools. The funds will be particularly targeted on children in disadvantaged areas who might not otherwise have access to the sort of facilities available in more affluent areas.

Improving opportunities for ethnic minority pupils

23. Children from ethnic minority backgrounds now represent one in ten of the school population, and over half a million of these do not have English as a first language. Investment of £430 million over the next three years will support the needs of children for whom English is an additional language and others at risk of failure, including support for community mentoring programmes for children. To enable schools to respond to these additional needs, they can receive grants to employ additional specialist teachers or bilingual classroom assistants. We are also implementing the Government's response to the Macpherson report to deal with racist incidents.

24. Following the White Paper *Excellence in schools* (July 1997, Cm 3681) we have now set in motion additional action, including consulting on how best to monitor ethnic minority pupils' performance and reviewing the level of specialist support and promoting the sharing of best practice.

25. Traveller children are particularly at risk of educational failure and social exclusion. We are determined that traveller children should have full access to education. A special grant programme supports additional funding of £13.5 million to provide a Traveller Education Service in some 130 LEAs in England. This programme is making significant progress in promoting attendance and increasing levels of achievement.

Improving opportunities for children with special educational needs

26. More effective provision for children with special educational needs (SEN) is a vital part of our strategy for raising standards overall, and promoting social inclusion. The Government's Programme of Action for SEN followed wide-ranging consultation on the Green Paper *Excellence for all children: Meeting Special Educational Needs* (October 1997, Cm 3785). This sets out the Government's key goals and how we intend to achieve them:

- improving support and advice for parents and carers of children with SEN;

- improving the existing framework for SEN, including the SEN Code of Practice, in particular to promote early intervention and more flexible delivery;

- enabling more children with SEN to be catered for in mainstream schools, while confirming and developing the role of special schools to support a locally inclusive system;

- investing in SEN training for education professionals and school governors; and

- promoting co-operation and effective partnership between schools, LEAs, health and social services and many other partners, to ensure effective delivery of services to children.

Improving educational opportunities for children across the United Kingdom

27. Policies are in place to raise standards in schools in all countries in the UK.

Northern Ireland

28. Some £54 million will be invested in the **School Improvement Programme** up to 2002. This includes the School Support Programme which is currently helping some 80 schools address their weaknesses and work towards self-improvement, by providing intensive professional support. It also includes strategies for the promotion of literacy and numeracy and for promoting and sustaining good behaviour in schools. It will impact on all schools, but most directly on schools and pupils in areas of social disadvantage. A further £22 million will be invested in the **Making a Good Start Initiative** which provides at least 10 hours a week classroom assistance for every Year 1 classroom. Together with the reduction in class sizes for pupils in Key Stage 1 this will secure the best possible start to education for all children.

Scotland

29. In Scotland, the White Paper *Targeting Excellence: Modernising Scotland's Schools* (January 1999, Cm 4247) sets out a broad strategy for raising standards, promoting social inclusion in schools and proposals for modernising the school system. The strategy contains a wide range of initiatives.

- **Early Intervention Programme.** We are investing £60 million over five years to support various projects designed to raise standards of literacy and numeracy in the early years of primary school so that children are then well-equipped to access all parts of the curriculum. Some authorities have focused Early Intervention projects on disadvantaged groups and, for many, a key focus is working in partnership with parents. And £23 million is being invested in **Alternatives to Exclusion,** a programme to help children remain in school. And all schools have set targets for improvement in exam performance, attendance, literacy and numeracy in the three-year period to 2001.

- **Study Support for schools.** Funds from the New Opportunities Fund and the Government's Excellence Fund will ensure study support and out-of-school learning throughout Scotland; and we are putting in place an action plan for improvement in provision for children with special educational needs.

- **Study Support outside schools.** We are developing and co-ordinating broadly-based educational support services delivered outside schools, through libraries, after-school clubs and homework centres, and we are improving access to facilities for children, offering them the opportunity to develop a range of life skills and interests.

- **New Community Schools.** We are providing funds of £26 million to support 60 pilot projects in all areas of Scotland (see Box 3.5).

30. The broad strategy set out in *Targeting Excellence* has been widely endorsed. The Scottish Executive has now published proposals for legislation to establish effective partnerships between schools, authorities, parents and central government to embed the continuous improvement in Scotland's school system.

New Community Schools is a radical initiative to modernise schools, raise attainment and promote social inclusion in Scotland. New Community Schools focus on the pupil and his or her family – addressing needs together by integrating the provision of formal and informal education, social work, family support and health education.

New Community Schools are to be piloted throughout Scotland with the aim of supporting at least two projects in each local authority by 2001. The first phase of the pilot is under way and involves 37 projects, encompassing over 150 schools. Although the first phase focuses on primary schools and schools serving deprived areas, the initiative is one which will have universal application. Two further phases will be funded, beginning in April 2000 and April 2001.

Seven of the pilots currently operating acted as Development Projects during 1998/99. One of these development projects used the resources allocated to support four main aims:

- raising attainment;

- lifelong learning;

- health; and

- support for families.

Activities undertaken included appointing a member of staff to facilitate and co-ordinate all the various elements of the project, building a new community centre office, establishing a crèche and a breakfast club, accommodating a money advice consultant, and running healthy exercise classes and various youth programmes for children and young people of all ages.

Personal Learning Plans will be piloted in New Community Schools because they are an essential structure to ensure that the needs and potential of children are fulfilled.

Wales

31.   *Pathway to Prosperity* (1998, Welsh Office) identifies ways to improve standards of education and training in line with the needs of the Welsh economy. The **Education and Training Action Group**, involving members from industry, education, business and the public sector, has been set up to produce an action plan to do this. Following consultation they will present the action plan to the National Assembly.

Box 3.6: Monitoring our progress

Ensuring that all children get a high-quality education wherever they go to school and providing additional help to children and their parents in the crucial pre-school years

Our indicators of success will track our progress in ensuring that all children are provided with a good basic start in life. We want to monitor our progress in improving the pre-school development of children in the most deprived areas, raising educational standards – especially literacy and numeracy   and tackling truancy and exclusions. We have also identified the key policy milestones we are putting in place to achieve these objectives.

Future policy milestones

- At least 250 local Sure Start programmes in England by 2001/02 and 100 per cent of families in contact with the local Sure Start programmes within the first two months of the birth of the child.

- To expand early years education provision for three-year-olds across the UK.

- Continued roll out of Education Action Zones.

- Maths Year 2000.

Indicators of success

- An increase in the proportion of seven-year-old Sure Start children achieving level 1 or above in the Key Stage 1 English and maths tests.

- Health outcomes in Sure Start areas:

   - a reduction in the proportion of low birth-weight babies in Sure Start areas; and

   - a reduction in the rate of hospital admissions as a result of serious injury in Sure Start areas.

- An increase in the proportion of those aged 11 achieving level 4 or above in the Key Stage 2 tests for literacy and numeracy.

- A reduction in the proportion of truancies and exclusions from school.

- An increase in the proportion of 19-year-olds with at least a level 2 qualification or equivalent.

Combating family poverty and social exclusion through our policies to tackle worklessness, increasing financial support for families and improving the environment in which children grow up

32.   The most important cause of disadvantage in childhood is living in a household where no one works. We are tackling this by breaking down the barriers that stop parents from working. We are providing increased financial support to those families when they most need it, when their children are young, through changes in the tax and benefits system. We are reforming Child Support so that more children receive support from both parents. And we are supporting families by improving housing and health and helping families deal with the pressures and challenges they face. These policies aim to ensure that children grow up in the best possible environment. They form the basis of our strategy to ensure that we create a society where no children live in poverty.

Tackling worklessness

33.   Worklessness is one of the most significant causes of child poverty. Six out of ten children with persistently low incomes live in workless households[36]. Lone parent families experience specific problems in combining work and caring for their families. Around six out of ten lone mothers do not work compared with one in three mothers with a partner, putting lone parents and their families at greater risk of low incomes[37]. Our policies aim to offer parents the support they need to enable them to combine work with caring for their children. They aim to remove the in-built disincentives within the tax and benefits system to ensure that work really pays.

34.   The measures which we have put in place to break down barriers preventing people from working and to improve work incentives are described in greater detail in **Chapter 4**, which looks at people of working age. But we highlight some key measures for families here.

- **The Working Families' Tax Credit** replaces Family Credit and will provide extra help to 1.5 million families from October 1999. It will generate a minimum income of £200 a week (£10,400 a year) to families with children with at least one full-time earner and ensure that work pays so that parents have a financial incentive to work.

- **Childcare tax credits** will build on the childcare disregard in Family Credit and will make childcare more affordable – the lowest earning families can now benefit. We are helping with 70 per cent of childcare charges up to a limit of £100 for families with one child and £150 for families with two children or more. The qualifying age will increase to cover all children up to age 15 and disabled children up to the age of 16. And a new clause in the Tax Credits Bill is intended to extend the range of eligible childcare for 8–14-year-olds.

- **Support for parents balancing work and family responsibilities:** we are legislating for a framework of family-friendly employee rights, including adoption of the European Working Time Directive governing working hours, and introduction of new parental leave rights. We plan to extend entitlement to Maternity Allowance to all women earning £30 a week or more. And, where the Government acts as employer, we will lead by example in promoting family-friendly employment practices, such as flexible working hours and job-sharing.

- **The New Deal for Lone Parents** (see Box 3.7). Over 80,000 lone parents have joined the New Deal and 21,000 have moved into jobs.

- **The National Childcare Strategy** (see paragraph 13).

Box 3.7: New Deal for Lone Parents

The New Deal is a comprehensive package of back-to-work help, designed to:

- help and encourage lone parents on Income Support to take up paid work; and

- improve the job-readiness of lone parents on Income Support and increase their employment opportunities.

Personal advisers offer help and advice with job search, training, childcare and in-work benefits. Up-to-date information on job vacancies is also available.

Over £190 million has been allocated over the lifetime of this Parliament from the Windfall Tax, including £10 million for in work training grants and innovative ideas from private and voluntary sectors for training.

Helping lone parents back into the job market.

Case study 3.6: Back to work with New Deal for Lone Parents

Susanna is a lone parent living in Sheffield. She has recently joined the New Deal for Lone Parents. She has a son aged $8^1/_2$ who is a special needs child. Susanna is claiming Income Support and receiving Invalid Care Allowance in addition to Disability Living Allowance. She is undergoing training through the Sheffield Chamber of Commerce, where she is gaining skills in computing, clerical work and report writing. She is working towards an NVQ in Business Administration and planning to take RSA typing exams. Susanna is currently on a work placement, as a clerical officer at a city centre hospital. Altogether Susanna is benefiting from a new sense of confidence and purpose in her life and is looking forward to becoming financially independent.

Increasing financial help for families bringing up children

35.	Families also need financial support to ensure that they have the resources they need to give children the best start in life. In Budget 98 and Budget 99 we provided significant increases in resources for families with children. Details of these measures are contained in Box 3.8. Reforms to the tax and benefits system will provide £6 billion a year in additional support for children by the end of this Parliament.

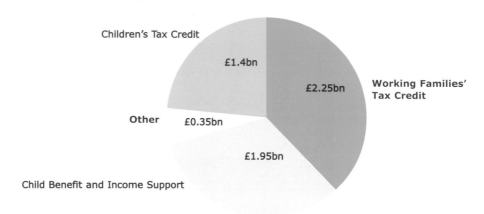

Chart 3.3: Composition of the additional £6 billion a year spent on new measures for children by the end of this Parliament

Source: Her Majesty's Treasury
Notes: 1. Based on estimates made for Budget 98 and Budget 99.
            2. A new Children's Tax Credit worth £416 off the tax bill of families with children will take effect from April 2001.

Reducing the number of children living in low-income households.

36.	Chart 3.4 (opposite) shows the total gains per week from the children's measures in the last two Budgets by position of the family in the income distribution. As a result of Budget 98 and Budget 99 measures, families with children will be on average £740 a year better off, and families with children in the poorest fifth will be on average £1,080 a year better off. As a result we would expect these measures to lead to a significant reduction in the numbers of children living in low-income households. We estimate that these measures will lift around 1.25 million people above half average income (equivalised by household), including 800,000 children. This is just an estimate of the direct impact of the budget measures – it does not take into account the effect on families who will be encouraged back to work because of the improved incentives to work.

37.	As Chart 3.4 (opposite) shows, all income groups will benefit as part of the Government's drive for a fairer tax system for families with children. The tax burden on a family with two children on average earnings will fall to its lowest level since 1972.

Help with the transition from welfare to work.

38.	In the Budget 99 we also announced that we are examining, for the longer term, the case for integrating the new Children's Tax Credit with the child premiums in Income Support and the Working Families' Tax Credit. This would build on Child Benefit and provide a single seamless system and a secure income to help the transition from welfare to work (see Box 3.8 opposite).

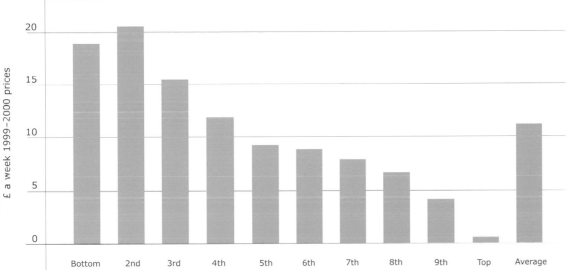

Chart 3.4: Impact of children's measures in Budget 98 and Budget 99 on the incomes of families with children by income decile

Increase in household net income, £ a week 1999-2000 prices

| Bottom | 2nd | 3rd | 4th | 5th | 6th | 7th | 8th | 9th | Top | Average |

Source: Her Majesty's Treasury
Note: Calculations based on estimates made for Budget 98 and Budget 99.

Box 3.8: Financial help for children from Budget 98 and Budget 99

Working Families' Tax Credit (commencing in October 1999 and to be uprated in April 2000)

- 1.5 million families will receive on average £24 a week more from Working Families' Tax Credit (WFTC) than from Family Credit – some families will gain over £45 a week. In addition, child maintenance will not affect the calculation of income for WFTC.

Children's Tax Credit (commencing April 2001)

- This will be worth up to £416 a year for families with children, compared with £198 for the Married Couple's Allowance.

Income Support

- The premiums for children aged under 11 will increase by £4.70 in October 1999 and by a further £1.05 in April 2000, bringing them into line with the premiums for children aged over 11. And we are allowing parents with care to keep more of their benefit when they receive child support maintenance – up to £10 a week.

Child Benefit

- Child Benefit for the first child was raised by £2.95 in April 1999 and will go up to £15 a week in April 2000 – an increase of 36 per cent since 1997. Child Benefit for second and subsequent children is being increased to £10 in April 2000.

Sure Start Maternity Grant

- In April 2000 the Sure Start Maternity Grant of £200 will replace the Social Fund Maternity Payment of £100.

We are also improving the position of young people with disabilities within the benefits system (see Box 3.9 overleaf).

- **Young people disabled before the age of 20** will be able to claim Incapacity Benefit. After a year on benefit, their entitlement will be £80.80 a week, compared with £54.40 a week at present on Severe Disablement Allowance – an extra £26.40 a week. A higher age limit of 25 will be introduced for those who begin training or higher education before the age of 20.

- **Three- and four-year-old severely disabled children** will get the higher rate mobility component of Disability Living Allowance, an extra £37 a week.

- **Disabled children's tax credit** – to be included in the Working Families' Tax Credit from October 2000 – will be worth at least £21.90 a week.

Reforming child support

39.   All children have the right to the financial support of both parents, wherever they live. Yet four out of five lone parents claiming Income Support receive no maintenance payments. The children living in families without this assistance are amongst the most disadvantaged of all. They suffer the low income associated with worklessness because their parents can be reluctant to take work without the guarantee of reliable income from child maintenance. The current system contains few incentives for lone parents claiming benefit to co-operate with the Child Support Agency (CSA):

- many parents do not trust the CSA system to treat them fairly; and

- one in three child support assessments takes more than six months to complete.

40.   Our White Paper, *A new contract for welfare: CHILDREN'S RIGHTS AND PARENTS' RESPONSIBILITIES* (July 1999, Cm 4349), sets out our plans for a new, straightforward, transparent and more customer-focused child support system built around:

- a simpler procedure. Parents will be able to work out how the maintenance has been calculated, and assessments will be made in a matter of weeks, rather than months as now;

- more effective methods of collection, with tough sanctions for those who do not co-operate; and

- the introduction of a maintenance premium in Income Support, allowing parents with care to keep more of their benefit when they receive child support maintenance – up to £10 a week.

Together these changes will help over one million children who do not receive financial support from non-resident parents.

Improving children's housing and health

41. As well as providing families with the financial support, we want to ensure that all children grow up in the best possible environment. Decent housing plays an important part in providing children and young people with a safe and healthy environment. Poor-quality housing can have negative impacts on health and in educational development.

42. We are investing **an additional £5 billion in housing** over the lifetime of this Parliament, which will help to improve and maintain existing social housing, provide new social housing and support renovation of private sector homes. Around two million homes will benefit from this extra investment.

43. Our consultation document *Fuel Poverty: The New Home Energy Efficiency Scheme* (May 1998, Department of the Environment, Transport and the Regions) sets out proposals for additional help with home energy efficiency for vulnerable people, including families on income-related benefits with young children. We propose to more than double the maximum grant from £315 to £700.

44. In Scotland, the Healthy Homes Initiative will tackle the dampness and condensation that affects many homes in Scotland. We aim to improve 100,000 homes through this initiative, giving priority to those on lower incomes. A key part of the Healthy Homes Initiative is the £12 million Warm Deal which will provide a comprehensive package of home energy efficiency. The scheme will create quality work experience and training opportunities for over 300 long-term unemployed people.

45. As well as good-quality housing, we want to improve children's health. The **Healthy Schools Programme** has set up pilot partnerships between education and health authorities to encourage healthy lifestyles among pupils. The lessons from the pilots will inform the launch of the national roll-out. A healthy school is one where good health and social behaviour underpin effective learning and academic achievement, which in turn promote long-term health gain. In Wales, the Better Health for Wales initiative is a strategy aimed at addressing a number of young people's health issues including smoking and sexual health.

A healthy school is one where good health and social behaviour underpin effective learning and academic achievement which in turn promotes long-term health gain.

> ### Case study 3.7: Mancunian Health Promotion Specialist Service
>
> This health promotion unit based in Manchester is providing a joint health and education initiative. It is a partnership between the LEA, health promotion services, advisory teachers and the police. It aims to improve the health of pupils by making sure they are better informed about issues such as smoking and drugs. An independent assessor has been appointed to work with schools themselves, to set health improvement targets and to monitor progress.

46. Children are more likely to have accidents. Accidental injury heads the league tables of causes of death among children and young people. It puts more children in hospital than any other cause. *Saving Lives: Our Healthier Nation* (July 1999, Cm 4386) outlines our programme of action to reduce the death rate from accidents by a least a fifth and serious injury by 10 per cent. We are funding the Child Accident Prevention Trust to pilot a special programme to reduce inequalities in children's injuries. A home accident-prevention strategy is being developed for publication in December 1999, to target children (and older people), particularly in deprived areas.

47. Social exclusion can be both a consequence of, and a contributory factor to, the development of mental health problems in children and young people. Economic pressures have their impact on family life and the secondary effects of parental depression, marital conflict and parental hostility, for instance, may impact upon children's emotional and behavioural development.

48. We aim to improve provision of appropriate, high-quality care and treatment for children and young people by building up locally-based Child and Mental Health Services (CAMHS). This should be achieved through improved staffing levels and training provision at all tiers and improved liaison between primary care, specialist CAMHS, social services and other agencies.

Supporting families

49. Our measures to improve children's housing and health are backed by a strategy of support to families which:

- recognises the central role which families play in our society; and

- takes practical steps to help and support parents and children to deal with the pressures and challenges which they face.

50. In the past, government departments did not work closely enough to develop a joined-up family policy or coherent practical initiatives to support families. We aim to address this through our cross-cutting **Supporting Families** initiative. This establishes the role of the State as playing an enabling role, putting children's interests first and supporting parents in the challenging role of bringing up children.

51. We are developing proposals in a wide range of areas including:

- **better services and support for parents:** all parents need support with their children's health and education. Many also want advice and support on bringing up children.

  ◆ We have already helped establish the new and independent National Family and Parenting Institute which will act as a centre of expertise providing guidance and developing better parenting support and a national telephone helpline for parents.

♦ We have also introduced a grant programme for voluntary organisations which provide services to support parents. Other measures include an expanded role for health visitors with greater emphasis on the prevention of problems and more help in the pre-school years.

52. The Scottish Executive has commissioned a research survey of projects or programmes across Scotland designed to offer support to parents or prospective parents. The final report is expected to identify gaps in current provision and help inform the development of a more strategic approach towards the development of parenting skills.

Box 3.10: Monitoring our progress

Combating family poverty and social exclusion through our policies to tackle worklessness, increasing financial support for families and improving the environment in which children grow up

We want to monitor our progress in improving children's lives. Our indicators will track our progress in helping parents work and raising the incomes of families with children and improving children's housing and health. We have also identified the key policy milestones – the introduction of the Working Families' Tax Credit and the new child support system that we need to meet as our reforms are implemented.

Future policy milestones

- Working Families' Tax Credit replaces Family Credit – **October 1999**.
- Children's Tax Credit – **April 2000**.

Indicators of success

- A reduction in the proportion of children living in workless households, for households of a given size, over the economic cycle.
- A reduction in the proportion of children in households with relatively low incomes.
- A reduction in the proportion of children in households with low incomes in an absolute sense.
- A reduction in the proportion of children in households with persistently low incomes.
- A reduction in the proportion of children living in poor housing.
- A reduction in the proportion of households with children experiencing fuel poverty.
- A reduction in the rate at which children are admitted to hospital as a result of an unintentional injury resulting in a hospital stay of longer than three days.

Supporting vulnerable young people, especially in the difficult transition from childhood to adult life

53. Most young people make the transition from childhood to adulthood smoothly. But too many do not. They may have failed at school – or school may have failed them. They may not have had the benefit of a supportive family; they may have had problems with drugs; they may have been drawn into crime. We want to tackle this disadvantage and give these young people the skills and knowledge they need to resist exclusion as adults. The goal of our policy for young people is that they should stay in education, training or work with a strong education/training component until they are aged at least 18.

54. Paragraph 6 outlined some of the key risk factors that hinder children as they move into adulthood. And in many cases they are interlinked in a cycle of cause and effect. Central to our bid to tackle poverty and social exclusion is to prevent these problems arising in the first place. One of the key events that can hinder children as they move into adulthood is teenage pregnancy.

Teenage pregnancy

55. Teenage parents are particularly vulnerable to the problems of poverty and social exclusion: they are less likely to finish their education, less likely to find a good job, and more likely to end up as single parents and bring up their children in poverty. We are committed to reducing the number of teenage conceptions and supporting this vulnerable group. The analysis and action on the Social Exclusion Unit's (SEU) report *Teenage Pregnancy* (June 1999, Cm 4342), to which the Government is now committed, are set out in Box 3.11 opposite.

Box 3.11: Teenage pregnancy

The UK has the highest teenage birth rate in Western Europe. In England there are nearly 90,000 teenage conceptions a year, including 2,200 to girls aged 14 or under.

The problem affects all areas, but is more serious in the poorest areas, and among the most vulnerable young people, including those in care and those who have been excluded from school.

In its report *Teenage Pregnancy* the SEU concluded that three major factors contribute to this:

- **low expectations** of education and job prospects;
- **ignorance** of contraception, relationships and what it means to be a parent; and
- **mixed messages from society** on attitudes to sexual activity and contraception.

The two main goals

- Reduce the rate of teenage conception, with the aim of halving the rate of conception among those under the age of 18 by 2010.
- Get more of those who are teenage parents, into education, training or employment, to reduce their risk of long-term social exclusion.

Measures to achieve these goals

- A National Campaign involving all sectors to improve understanding and change behaviour.
- Joined-up action at national and local level to manage the strategy and ensure it is on track.
- Prevention – action to tackle the causes of teenage pregnancy, including better education, access to contraception, and a new focus on young men, in service design.
- Better support for teenage parents, including helping them return to school to complete education, and piloting new support packages to help with housing, healthcare, parenting skills and childcare.

56. In Scotland, over 9,000 teenage girls become pregnant each year – more than 40 in every 1,000. The **Healthy Respect** scheme aims to address this by fostering responsible sexual behaviour among young people, concentrating on preventing unwanted teenage pregnancies and sexually transmitted diseases. In Northern Ireland, teenage pregnancy is one of four priority issues tackled under the Promoting Social Inclusion initiative designed to help the most disadvantaged people.

Fostering responsible sexual behaviour among young people.

> ### Case study 3.8: Newpin Teenage Mum's Project, Peckham
>
> This project works with young mothers and their children to encourage constructive family behaviour; to provide opportunities for positive parenting; to raise levels of self-esteem; and to increase the educational and employment opportunities available to young mothers. The project offers:
>
> - a Parent Support Group meeting weekly to share advice on looking after both their children and themselves;
>
> - a Personal Development Programme to help young mothers prepare for return to school, further education or employment, including providing basic skills tuition in English and maths;
>
> - a telephone support line for emergency advice and reassurance around the clock; and
>
> - practical support with, for example, budgeting and shopping, and communicating with different support systems such as housing, social services and benefits.

Education and training after the age of 16

57.   Britain has a smaller share of 17–18-year-olds in full-time education than any other industrialised nation. Worse still, at any one time, 160,000 16–18-year-olds (9 per cent of the age group) are not in learning or work. Those with a background of educational underachievement and disaffection, and family disadvantage and poverty, are at particular risk of falling into this group. In some areas, non-participation is considerably higher than the national average among some members of ethnic minority groups and other disadvantaged groups. There are strong links between non-participation and outcomes which are costly for both the individuals and society as a whole – unemployment, benefit dependency, teenage parenthood, offending, substance misuse, homelessness and mental illness.

Box 3.12: The Beattie Committee

The Government set up the Beattie Committee in April 1998 to examine post-school transitions for young people who have additional support needs in Scotland, including those with physical and mental disabilities and those who are at risk of social exclusion. The Committee has taken evidence from a very wide range of professionals in this field and has listened to young people themselves. The report of the Committee, which puts inclusiveness at the heart of its recommendations, has now been published. An action plan will be published early in 2000.

58. We are committed to a strategy of improving outcomes for 16–18-year-olds. The SEU's report *Bridging the Gap: New Opportunities for 16–18-year-olds not in education, employment or training* (July 1999, Cm 4405) sets out the foundations for our strategy for this age group (see Box 3.13).

Box 3.13: Improving outcomes for 16–18-year-olds

The main elements of the SEU's report are:

- a clear outcome to aim for by the age of 19 (graduation) which suits the needs of all young people. The Qualifications and Curriculum Authority has been asked to develop and consult on options;

- a variety of pathways to 'graduation' which suit the needs of all young people. The principles for effective post-16 learning are set out for incorporation in funding, inspection and professional development;

- building on the Education Maintenance Allowance pilots to engage the most disadvantaged groups, and a youth card to assist with transport and other costs; and

- a new multi-skill support service, working with all young people, but giving priority to those most at risk of underachievement and disaffection, to support them between the ages of 13–19 through education and the transition to adulthood.

59. These recommendations are being taken forward in our new **ConneXions** strategy. ConneXions encourages young people to stay in learning until the age of 19 to help them achieve at least a level 2, or equivalent qualification. It will build on current initiatives, to improve participation and achievement in learning. And it will concentrate on:

- identifying innovative ways of tackling disaffection among 14–17-year-olds through New Start;

Support and
guidance to
raise
aspirations
for young
people.

- ensuring young people have the help, support and guidance that will raise their aspirations and tackle any personal and family problems standing in their way. From September 1999, we are introducing a Learning Gateway for 16–17-year-olds who need extra guidance and support to benefit from mainstream learning;

- encouraging employees aged 16–17, who did not achieve good qualifications at school, to take advantage of the new right to study for approved qualifications;

- ensuring that the range of qualifications and courses is attractive and motivating, both to individuals and employers;

- building on the best work being done in schools, in colleges and in work-based training to drive up quality and standards across all modes of learning; and

- tackling barriers to learning, including financial barriers. We are piloting Educational Maintenance Allowances in 15 LEAs. These pilots will target financial support to young people from low-income families who might otherwise be excluded from learning.

60. We recognise the importance to young people gaining a wide range of social skills so that they can fully participate in society. Schools will play an important role in ensuring young people acquire the skills and knowledge they need to resist exclusion as adults. They will offer opportunities for all their pupils to develop personally and socially; to develop confidence, positive self-esteem and be able to look after their health and well-being; and to maintain worthwhile and fulfilling relationships. Proposals for a national framework for Personal, Social and Health Education and Citizenship in schools will be published in the autumn of 1999.

Case study 3.9: Merseyside New Start project

A programme in Toxteth, within the **Merseyside New Start** project, provides an alternative curriculum for young people excluded from or not attending school. One young girl, who came from a background where none of her family had ever worked, undertook a work placement in a florist shop which helped her to understand the value of work and consider future career opportunities. She now has a Saturday job and plans to attend college.

61. In Wales the Youth Access, Youth Gateway and Youth Pathfinder programmes will work with disaffected 16–18-year-olds not in education, work or training.

Helping children looked after by local authorities

62. We know that these children are particularly vulnerable and face multiple disadvantage. It is vital for them to participate in education and training after the age of 16, but they are likely to need extra support in the transition from childhood to adult life.

63. In 1998, 7,900 young people aged 16 and over left care. Their life chances are significantly worse than their peers': as many as 75 per cent of care leavers have no educational qualifications; up to 50 per cent are unemployed; and up to 20 per cent experience some form of homelessness within two years of leaving care. Of those leaving care, 20 per cent are likely to become homeless at some stage in the following two years.

64. We have a wide range of measures to improve services for care leavers including:

   - extending the statutory responsibilities on local authorities to support these young people; improving the quality of the care system so that they are better prepared for adulthood;

   - issuing guidance on good practice;

   - improving measures for care leavers to obtain suitable and affordable accommodation; and

   - our three-year **Quality Protects Programme** which will modernise the delivery of children's social services in England. Through Quality Protects, the Department of Health will be supporting local authorities with the implementation of these objectives. For children being looked after by social services in particular, we want to see improved educational attainment, better health and development, and reduced levels of offending (see Box 3.14).

As many as 75% of care leavers have no educational qualifications; up to 50% are unemployed; and up to 20% experience some form of homelessness within two years of leaving care.

Improving life chances of young people leaving care.

Box 3.14: Quality Protects

The main elements are:

- new Government objectives for children's services which set clear outcomes for children;

- an important role for elected councillors in delivering the programme set out in new guidance;

- new children's services' special grant of £375 million over three years; and

- eight teams of Regional Development Workers to support local authorities.

All local authorities have drawn up a Quality Protects Management Action Plan setting out their strategy for the next three years. Their progress will be closely monitored by the Department of Health.

65. One of Quality Protects' key objectives is to improve the life chances of young people leaving care. We issued the consultation paper *Me, Survive, Out There?* (July 1999, Department of Health) setting out proposals for new arrangements for young people living in and leaving care (see Box 3.15).

Box 3.15: Young people living in and leaving care

Me, Survive, Out There? sets out proposals for the future to ensure:

- local authorities look after young people until they are ready to leave care;

- there is better preparation for leaving care; and

- when young people leave care, they get the support they need.

Main elements

- extending the statutory responsibilities on local authorities to support these young people;

- each young person to have a 'pathway plan' mapping out clear pathways to independence and a Young Person's Adviser co-ordinating the provision of support and assistance; and

- new resources for support and assistance of 16–17-year-olds who are in care or who have left care.

66. In Northern Ireland, each Health and Social Services Board has recently published a **Children's Services Plan** which sets out how the Board will co-operate with other agencies and organisations to promote the welfare of vulnerable children and young people, including those leaving care.

67. In Scotland, the Social Inclusion Partnership initiative (in which partnership groups can bid to deliver regeneration programmes in deprived areas) will include schemes to improve the help available to young people who have left care. A Children's Services Development Fund is providing £37 million over three years to ensure expansion of foster care services, greater advocacy for children looked after away from home, and increased support for families with very young children.

68. In Wales, the Children First programme will deliver similar improvements in the management and delivery of children's services and better outcomes for looked-after children and children in need. £5 million has been made available in the local authority revenue settlement for Wales this year to support implementation of this programme.

Youth offending

69. We know that disadvantaged children, particularly those with poor levels of education, are more likely to offend. We want to prevent this and we want to deter repeat offending. This will improve the long-term prospects of young people who have become involved in crime and also improve the quality of the environment in some of the most deprived areas of the country.

> Interventions to deal with young people at risk of offending.

70. Tackling youth crime is one of our core pledges. Juveniles make up a quarter of all known offenders. In the past, the criminal justice system has failed to deal effectively with them. Too often, they have offended while awaiting trial; too often, they have gone on to become habitual offenders. We have taken powers in the Crime and Disorder Act to ensure that the young offenders of today do not become the career criminals of tomorrow, and to involve parents in this process.

71. The new Youth Justice Board is charged with monitoring the operation of the youth justice system and promoting good practice, including a range of new interventions to deal with young people at risk of offending and to tackle the problems of those who have started offending. New local Youth Offending Teams bring together the expertise of the probation, social, prison, health and education services.

72. And the SEU report *Bridging the Gap* outlines our commitment to substantial improvements in the education and training of offenders, in particular that offenders aged under 18 in custody will receive a minimum of 30 hours a week of education or training.

> Youth Action Groups increase young people's interest in, and awareness of, crime prevention, and give them a sense of social responsibility.

73. Youth groups can play an important role in steering young people away from crime and other anti-social behaviour. In 1993, the Prudential Corporation and Crime Concern launched a five-year strategy, worth some £1.25 million, to develop youth crime prevention panels – Youth Action Groups – in all secondary schools in the country, encouraging young people to tackle problems of relevance to them. There are now over 1,200 Youth Action Groups. They work to increase young people's interest in, and awareness of, crime prevention, and give them a sense of social responsibility.

Case study 3.10: Dalston Youth Project

The **Dalston Youth Project** in London targets high-risk young offenders aged 11–18. Its key feature is a community mentoring scheme which aims to encourage and support young people to return to education and training. In 1998 it received a Certificate of Special Commendation at the Crime Concern European Crime Prevention Awards.

The Project's first programme, for 30 young people, began in 1994 and it has helped some 50 young people each year since then. More than 80 per cent of the young people who join have a criminal record.

- 70 per cent of the 15–18-year-olds have gone on to college, others have gone on to training or a job.

- More than 60 per cent do not re-offend in the year after they leave the Project.

Case study 3.11: The Freagarrach Project

The **Freagarrach Project** (run by Barnardos) delivers active interventions to 12–16-year-olds using a cognitive behavioural approach aimed at addressing offending. To be evaluated over five years, initial findings indicate that re-offending rates have been cut by over 60 per cent in relation to previous offending patterns.

Case study 3.12: The Children and Youth Partnership Fund

The **Children and Youth Partnership Fund**, launched in April 1999 as part of the Social Inclusion Fund for Wales, aims to promote local initiatives to lift children's educational achievement, engage them in creative activities in their communities and deter them from crime, drugs, vandalism and truancy. It seeks to encourage young people and children to strive for independence and to develop a sense of community and personal achievement.

Box 3.16: Monitoring our progress

Supporting vulnerable young people, especially in the difficult transition from childhood to adult life

Our indicators of success will monitor our progress in helping all children make a successful transition to adulthood. We want to improve educational and training outcomes for 16–18-year-olds, to make a substantial reduction in teenage conceptions and to improve outcomes for those leaving local authority care. We have also identified the key policy milestones that we need to meet in order to make a real difference to young people's lives.

Future policy milestones

- Further Education Maintenance Allowance pilots in **September 2000**.

- Youth Support Service – national arrangements from **autumn 2000**, with local services in place from **April 2001**.

- Introduce teenage pregnancy recommendations:

  - new guidance on sex education will be issued by the Department for Education and Employment for consultation by **summer 2000**;

  - guidance on criteria for the provision of effective and responsible youth contraception and advice services will be issued by the Department of Health by **summer 2000**; and

  - pilot of a new programme of co-ordinated support for pregnant teenagers and teenage parents aged under 18, in 20 areas for three years from **April 2000**.

Indicators of success

- A reduction in the proportion of 16–18-year-olds not in education or training.

- An improvement in the educational attainment of children looked after by local authorities.

- Teenage pregnancy:

  - a reduction in the rate of conceptions for those aged under 18; and

  - an increase in the proportion of those who are teenage parents, in education, employment or training.

Involving children and young people in policy development

74. This chapter can only give a brief overview of the range of work which is under way to tackle the complex problems of child poverty and social exclusion. We continue to work with statutory and voluntary organisations concerned with young people, to help us to better understand and tackle the causes of the problems. These are examples of opportunities that young people have had to speak about issues and policies that affect their lives.

Box 3.17: Involving children and young people

- **The Real Deal** – a project being carried out by Pilotlight, Centrepoint, Save the Children, the Camelot Foundation and Demos to consult groups of disadvantaged young people across the country. In December 1998 a workshop involving young people and senior policy makers was held at Downing Street.

- The **SEU's** *Bridging the Gap* report drew heavily on research with discussion groups of particularly disadvantaged young people, and its emerging conclusions were tested out on some of the young people brought together by the Real Deal.

- Small **consultative groups** were set up across Scotland in 1998 to inform a report on the views of children and young people on the impact of the UN Convention on the Rights of the Child on their own lives. Details of the exercise were published in July 1999 by Save the Children, Scotland in their report *Our Lives*.

- The **Youth Council for Northern Ireland** is undertaking a comprehensive study to produce guidelines whereby young people can become engaged in active dialogue with policy makers on issues which affect their lives. Detailed research is currently under way looking at case studies of best practice.

75. Finding ways in which children and young people can influence the design and delivery of policy is one of the main issues being looked at by Policy Action Team 12 on Young People, as part of the SEU's programme to tackle problems requiring cross-Whitehall solutions. This Team will report in December 1999.

4 People of working age

Helping people back to work

Economic prosperity and social justice depend on people of working age being able to realise their potential in the labour market. The proportion of working-age households where no one has a job has doubled since 1979; the majority of these are trapped on low incomes.

We want to improve opportunities to work, to learn and to increase earning potential; and to give individuals the tools they need to help themselves. But the difficulties go beyond low income and worklessness. We want to tackle discrimination, improve the effectiveness of public services and provide a more inclusive society for all people of working-age.

Here we set out our strategy to tackle the problems faced by people of working-age. We are:

- building a proactive welfare system to help people into work;

- making work pay;

- promoting lifelong learning to ensure people have the skills and education to respond to the modern labour market; and

- supporting vulnerable groups and those most at risk of discrimination and disadvantage.

THE PROBLEM

1. Worklessness is the main cause of poverty and social exclusion. Of all working-age adults 13 per cent now live in workless households[1], one of the highest rates in Europe[2]. Lack of work leads to low incomes: six out of ten low-income adults live in households where no one works; this compares with fewer than one in ten who live in a household where all adults are in work (see Chart 4.1). This is not only wrong, but also a huge waste in economic terms. Improving employment opportunities for this group will increase the productive potential of the economy, leading to benefits for society as a whole.

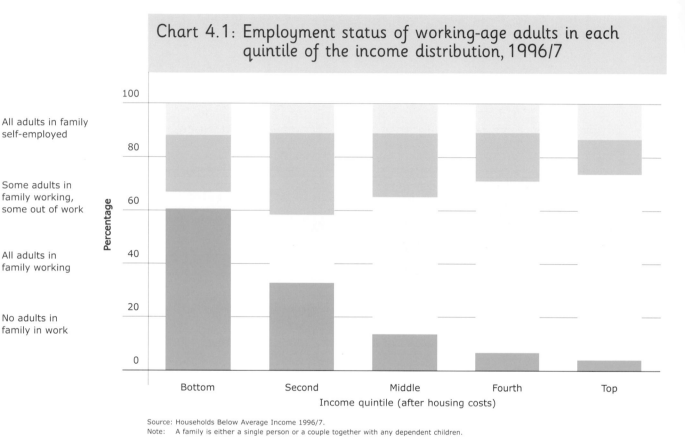

Chart 4.1: Employment status of working-age adults in each quintile of the income distribution, 1996/7

All adults in family self-employed

Some adults in family working, some out of work

All adults in family working

No adults in family in work

Source: Households Below Average Income 1996/7.
Note: A family is either a single person or a couple together with any dependent children.

2. The most important routes out of low income are finding a job, keeping a job and moving up the earnings distribution out of low-paid work. Almost two out of three low-income people who move out of low income do so because someone in the household gets a job or increases their earnings[3]. Being in work provides additional advantages apart from financial well-being such as a sense of purpose and increased self-esteem[4].

3. We have identified three major barriers preventing people from returning to work and improving their earnings when in work.

- **Long periods out of work and a 'low-pay, no-pay cycle'.** Five million people of working-age are claiming out-of-work benefits and three million have been claiming for more than two years[5]. The longer people are out of work the less likely it is that they will return to work[6], because they can lose skills and motivation, their health may deteriorate or because employers may be unwilling to recruit people without recent work experience. Spells out of work tend to reduce people's earnings potential when in work[7], and those who are low paid tend to be more likely to lose their jobs subsequently so people can get trapped into a 'low-pay, no-pay' cycle[8]. Long periods out of work can have an impact on people's prospects in the future – the experience can 'scar' people. On average, men who before the age of 23 had been unemployed for 12 months or more, were out of work for ten times longer in the following decade than those who had never been unemployed[9].

- **Lack of skills.** In today's dynamic labour market, having the skills to compete effectively is crucial. As Chart 4.2 shows, only half of women and men with no qualifications are in work compared with over 80 per cent of those with A level and above qualifications. Men with very low literacy and numeracy skills are about six times more likely to be out of work than those with good skills[10]. Between 20 and 25 per cent of adults in Britain have poor literacy and numeracy skills[11]. And increased skills are key to improving incomes for those in work as well. Adults without any educational qualifications are twice as likely to be trapped on low incomes as those with degrees[12].

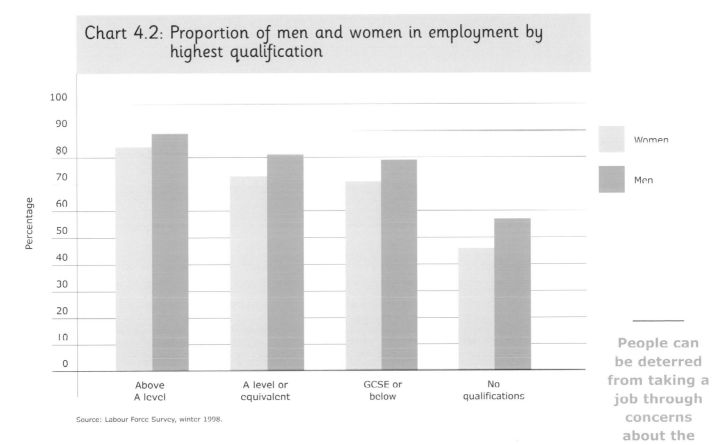

Chart 4.2: Proportion of men and women in employment by highest qualification

Source: Labour Force Survey, winter 1998.

- **Disincentives to work.** This is a particular problem for families with children, especially young children. Lack of affordable, high quality childcare can make it difficult for parents, especially lone parents, to work (see Chart 4.3 overleaf). For some, a poor knowledge of in-work benefits can lead people to misjudge the gains from work[13]. People can

People can be deterred from taking a job through concerns about the security of their income stream in work.

be deterred from taking a job through concerns about the security of their income stream in work[14]. Others are concerned about accepting low-paid jobs as they worry about not being able to cope until the first pay day[15]. And there is evidence that, for some, the costs involved with job search can limit their searching activity[16].

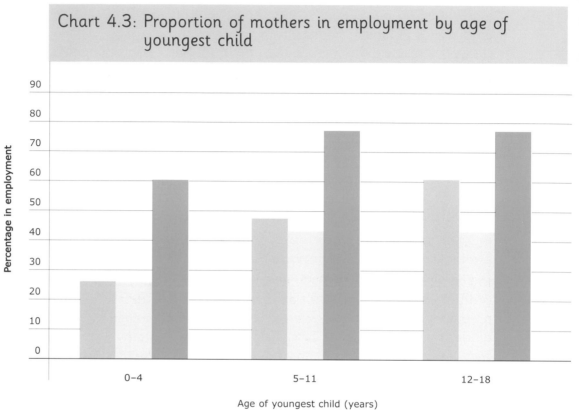

Chart 4.3: Proportion of mothers in employment by age of youngest child

Legend:
Lone mothers

Mothers with an unemployed partner

Mothers with an employed partner

Percentage in employment

Age of youngest child (years)

Source: Labour Force Survey, winter 1998.

4. However, for some people of working age, earning a living is not a realistic prospect, at least not in the short term. Many working-age people suffer from linked problems of poor health, disability, poor housing and poor environments. For example, many homeless people face a 'no-home, no-job' cycle and may need substantial help before they are in a position to find work. Some people who are long-term sick and some people with a disability may not be in a position to seek work. They need security and opportunities to live active and fulfilling lives. Carers make a significant contribution to society but this too often goes unrecognised. Many people are denied opportunities because of their gender, their age, their ethnic origin or their disability (see Box 4.1).

Box 4.1: Disadvantaged groups

- **Lone parents**, most of whom are women, are heavily concentrated at the lower end of the income distribution. In the UK just over 40 per cent of lone mothers work (see Chart 4.3) – much lower than the proportion in many other European countries. And most working lone parents work part-time and have relatively low earnings. Lone mothers are much less likely to be qualified than other mothers and the long periods they spend out of work tend to erode the skills they have.

- **The partners of unemployed people** are significantly less likely to be in employment than the partners of the employed. Chart 4.3 shows that a woman with a working partner is twice as likely to be in work as a woman whose partner is not working. Some of this difference is due to differences in characteristics – lack of skills and local labour market conditions – but some of the difference can be attributed to disincentives in the benefits system[17].

- **People with a long-term illness or disability**. The economic activity rate for people of working age with a long-term disability (51 per cent) is substantially less than for those without a disability (86 per cent)[18]. People with a long-term illness or disability face problems of reduced ability and motivation, employer discrimination, outdated skills, and poor availability of suitable employment. Those with mental health problems are particularly likely to be socially excluded.

- **Older men coming up to retirement age** have increasingly dropped out of the labour market. In 1979 around one in five men aged 55–65 years was not working. By 1997 this proportion had doubled[19]. In some cases this fall reflects increasing numbers of people taking voluntary early retirement, with access to a good income stream from an occupational pension. But for many this 'early retirement' is involuntary and leads to low income. Employment rates for older women (aged 55–60) have not declined in the same way, but they have not risen – unlike the rates for younger women.

- **People from ethnic minorities**. People from some ethnic minorities are significantly more likely to be out of work than White people[20]. Differences in the level of qualifications cannot adequately explain these differences; for example unemployment rates are higher for people from ethnic minority groups no matter what their level of qualification[21]. Ethnic minority men are more likely to have experienced unemployment than White men during their working lives. In a recent survey, 13 per cent of ethnic minority men aged under 35 had spent more than a third of their working lives unemployed compared with just 7 per cent of White men. Around half of younger ethnic minority men had, since the age of 16, spent more than a third of their working lives in unemployment[22].

(continued)

Women with a working partner are twice as likely to be in work as a woman whose partner is not working.

Unemployment rates are higher for people from ethnic minority groups no matter what their level of qualification.

- **People on the margins** such as rough sleepers or those with drug problems are perhaps the most disadvantaged. They often suffer from multiple problems: for example 30–50 per cent of rough sleepers suffer from mental health problems, as many as 50 per cent have a serious alcohol problem and some 20 per cent misuse drugs[23].

How did we get into this position?

5. Today's labour market is very different from 50 years ago when the Welfare State was in its infancy. We have had to face increased structural unemployment along with an increasingly competitive global economy. This has been accompanied by economic growth and technological innovation and a shift away from unskilled and semi-skilled work to skilled work and more diverse forms of employment – in particular, more part-time jobs, short-term contracts and self-employment. These changes have been accompanied by changes in family structure, and a greater tendency for women to work (see Chart 4.4).

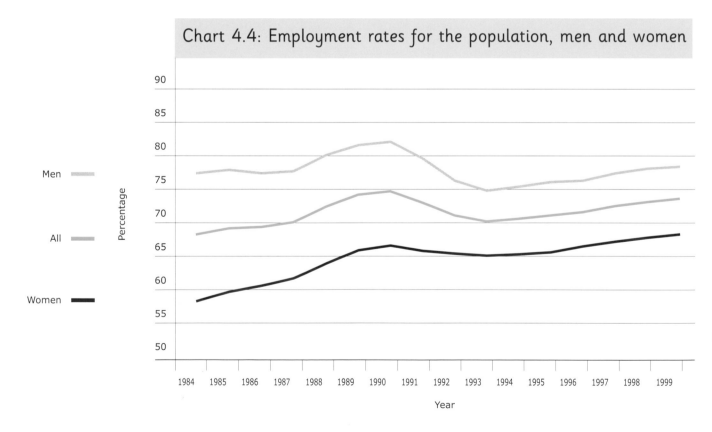

Chart 4.4: Employment rates for the population, men and women

Source: Labour Force Survey, spring of each year.

6. Employment rates are nearly as high as they have ever been. But the distribution of employment opportunities has not been shared equally either between households or geographically. The proportion of working-age households where no one has a job has more than doubled since 1979 (see Chart 4.5). The growth in workless households has been driven by the decline in male employment rates but also by an increase in the numbers of single adult households, including lone parent households. In addition, work has become increasingly unevenly distributed across households as the rise in women's employment has been concentrated in households where someone is already in work.

Employment rates are nearly as high as they have ever been. But the distribution of employment opportunities has not been shared equally.

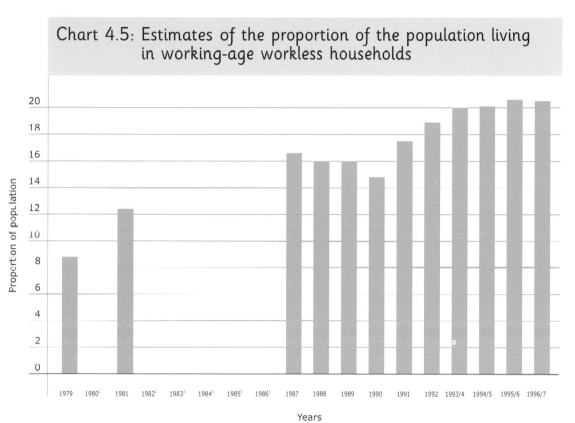

Chart 4.5: Estimates of the proportion of the population living in working-age workless households

Proportion of population

Years

Source: Households Below Average Income (HBAI) Family Expenditure Survey.
Notes: 1 HBAI data not available for 1980 and 1982–86.

7. The composition of the working-age workless population has also changed.

- The proportion of workless households headed by a lone parent has increased. Increasing numbers of working-age people have become reliant on sickness, incapacity and disability benefits.

- The number of working-age people claiming long-term sickness and incapacity benefits increased fivefold between 1972 and 1999[24]. Of the five million working-age claimants on out-of-work benefits, half are claiming benefits because they are sick or disabled and one in five is claiming because they are a lone parent[25].

Breaking
down the
barriers faced
by all those
locked out of
the labour
market.

8. Past policies have also contributed to the problems. The Welfare State has failed to evolve quickly enough to keep pace with economic and social shifts. Help in getting back into work was concentrated on the unemployed claimant rather than on all groups who could benefit such as partners of the unemployed. The benefits system concentrated on passively paying out benefits, rather than providing active support and a route back into work. We want to provide new opportunities and break down the barriers faced by all groups locked out of the labour market – lone parents, people with a long-term illness or disability as well as the unemployed claimant.

WHAT WE ARE DOING – OUR POLICY PRIORITIES

Long and
severe
downturns in
the economy
have led to
large numbers
of people
experiencing
long spells out
of the labour
market where
they lose the
skills and
motivation to
benefit from
the upturn in
the labour
market.

9. Economic growth, opportunity and fairness go hand in hand: an economy in which a significant proportion of the population is unable to fulfil its potential will be a poorer and less productive one. Stable sustainable economic growth is crucial in combating poverty and social exclusion. The boom and bust cycle experienced in the past has inflicted immense damage on the labour market. Long and severe downturns in the economy have led to large numbers of people experiencing long spells out of the labour market where they lose the skills and motivation to benefit from the upturn in the labour market. New monetary and fiscal policies have been put in place to ensure sustained, non-inflationary growth. Economic growth, together with effective policies to help people into work, make work pay and raise skills through lifelong learning, form the basis of our strategy.

10. But we need to go further, to build a fairer society where people are not marginalised because of their gender, ethnic origin, their age, or because they have a disability. Some groups in society can suffer discrimination or find that, for other reasons, they are denied fair access to key public services or are marginalised from mainstream society. And we need to do more for the minority of working-age people for whom work is not an option.

Building a proactive welfare system to help people into work

11. Our strategy is to tackle the causes of poverty and social exclusion by helping people find work. We are reforming the welfare state to help those with greatest need. We are changing our approach: developing new ways to remove barriers to work and to break the cycle of dependency and insecurity.

ONE and the New Deal

12. A proactive welfare system is at the heart of tackling worklessness. Our ambition is to deliver a change of culture among benefit claimants, employers and public servants, with rights and responsibilities on all sides. Those making the shift from welfare into work are being provided with positive assistance, not just a benefit payment. We are shifting the focus to include all groups – partners of the unemployed, lone parents, carers, people with a long-term illness or disability – not just the claimant unemployed. There are two key components to this.

13. **ONE.** The starting point for ONE is that the emphasis for almost all people when first claiming benefit should be on returning to work. New benefit clients of working age, including carers, lone parents and people with disabilities, will be required to take part in work-focused interviews.

> *A proactive welfare system is at the heart of tackling worklessness.*

- ONE is a crucial part of our welfare reform agenda. It is about helping people access work related opportunities. A single point of entry into the system will help us forge a new culture that puts work first and is based on a seamless, flexible and modern service for all clients.

- In ONE, all people of working age making a claim to benefit will have access to, and be expected to take advantage of the same service (subject to flexibilities for the terminally ill or recently bereaved, for example). The personal adviser service will help benefit claimants of working-age find ways in which they can overcome barriers that prevent participation in the labour market, and help individuals gain access to a range of services, such as childcare provision, specialist counselling and housing support.

- It will offer individuals an allocated personal adviser who can help them, whatever their needs might be, to move into independence through work where they can. We have evidence from the New Deals that personal advisers can have a positive and powerful impact. Relatively simple advice can be surprisingly effective.

- ONE is being piloted in a total of twelve areas. Four started in June 1999, with plans for a further eight from November 1999. The ONE pilots have received £79.5 million from the Government's Invest to Save budget. ONE will involve closer working between the Benefits Agency and the Employment Service. From April 2000 (subject to legislation) a requirement to take part in a personal adviser interview will be introduced to all pilots.

14. **The New Deals.** We are providing additional support for those who have been out of work for some time or, as in some cases, where people have very little or no experience of work. Some of this group will be demotivated, some will have lost confidence in their social skills, some will need reskilling – but for most the pathway back to the mainstream is through experiencing work and the workplace. The New Deal, funded by the Windfall Tax, is the largest ever investment in getting people into work. At its heart lies the simple proposition that the vast majority of workless people have the potential to earn their own living but in the early days of getting back to work, or becoming self-employed, both employee and employer need positive help. The New Deal is based around a personal adviser. The personal adviser is able to identify and overcome the specific barriers individuals face in trying to move from welfare into work. The programme, which is run on a partnership basis, including business, has six schemes.

- **New Deal for Young People** is a £2.6 billion programme for 18–24-year-olds who have been unemployed for six months or more. The programme has been running throughout the UK since April 1998 and offers four options:

◆ a job for which an employer receives a subsidy of £60 a week, or help to become self-employed;

◆ full-time education and training;

◆ a job with a voluntary organisation; or

◆ a job with the Environment Task Force.

The job options last for six months and full-time education and training can last for up to one year. By the end of June 1999 over 300,000 young people had joined the programme and 123,000 of these had entered jobs (91,000 had been working for 13 weeks or more).

Case study 4.1: New Deal for Young People in Brighton and Hove

Brighton, despite its apparent affluence, has areas of severe deprivation and many disadvantaged and socially excluded people. In 1998, the Employment Service New Deal team and Brighton and Hove Council social services department developed and ran a trial project that offered disadvantaged young people work-based opportunities through the New Deal employment option. The 18 young people on the first trial project, the majority of whom had few, if any, qualifications and some of whom were homeless, were employed for six months with a supportive employer (the local social services department) who understood their problems and would help them to transfer from a supported environment into the world of work. Fifteen young people completed the project and more than 50 per cent of these moved on to permanent employment. The scheme has been extended to offer up to 80 places throughout 1999 and the first half of 2000.

● **New Deal for the Long-term Unemployed aged 25 and over** is a £0.5 billion investment in adults who have been unemployed for two years or more. This New Deal provides job subsidies of £75 a week for six months and opportunities for full-time education or training for up to one year. At the end of June 1999, 150,700 people joined this programme and 19,000 had found jobs (16,000 of them had been working for 13 weeks or more).

- **New Deal for the Over-50s** is an important new package of back-to-work help being introduced with £250 million government funds over the next three years. It will include a cash employment credit of £60 a week paid for up to one year for those people or their dependent partners entering full-time employment (£40 for part-time work) who are aged 50 or over and have been out of work and on benefits for more than six months. It will offer employment guidance from a personal adviser, job search support and a training subsidy. It will also apply to self-employment. Pathfinders (regions to pilot new ways of working) will be in place from October 1999 and the programme will be introduced nationally by early 2000.

  - In addition, the **Active Ageing Project** being undertaken by the Performance and Innovation Unit for the Inter-Ministerial Group for Older People will address some of these concerns. The project will assess the implications of the trend towards economic inactivity of people aged between 50 and 65 and identify whether the Government should take further action to enable them to remain in economic activity or to participate in other worthwhile activities (such as volunteering and lifelong learning). The project will report to the Prime Minister in autumn 1999.

- **New Deal for Partners of the Unemployed (NDPU)** started with a £60 million voluntary scheme that allows partners aged 25 or over who have been unemployed for six months the help they need to get back to work. Partners aged 18–24 without children have the opportunity to be included voluntarily in the New Deal for Young People. NDPU will also introduce joint claims for Jobseeker's Allowance. Childless couples where initially one or both is aged 18–24, will both be required to become job seekers. Those aged 18–24 will go on to New Deal for Young People. Exemptions will be available to accommodate those who cannot meet JSA conditions (for example, because of caring responsibilities, incapacity or full-time study). Joint claims will be introduced from October 2000 at the earliest.

- **New Deal for Disabled People** is a £195 million joint initiative between the Department of Social Security and the Department for Education and Employment to test ways of improving opportunities for people with disabilities who want to move into or stay in work. One key element of the New Deal involves funding a number of innovative schemes to test ways of helping people who want to work. Ten contracts were awarded in July 1998 and further contracts were announced in spring 1999.

- **New Deal for Lone Parents** which is described in **Chapter 3**.

Case study 4.2: New Deal for Disabled People in Wales

This innovative scheme, called Disability Business Partnerships, is run by a consortium of local organisations including RNIB, SCOPE, regional TECs and local business organisations.

The scheme aims to help people with disabilities into work or training with a particular focus on the needs of local ethnic minority groups. Since the scheme began, over 100 people with disabilities have been helped to find work, to join work experience or to start training.

15. In addition to ONE and the New Deals, from April 2000 we will launch Employment Zones (EZs). Further details on EZs are in **Chapter 6**.

Helping the long-term unemployed reintegrate

16. ONE and the New Deal build on the success of the Employment Service (see Box 4.2) which places about 1.3 million people into jobs annually. Of these, 200,000 are long-term unemployed and about 100,000 are people with disabilities.

Box 4.2: Employment Service

The Employment Service offers a range of programmes to help people back into work.

- **Travel to Interview Scheme**. Assistance for those who have been unemployed for over 13 weeks in order to attend job interviews for permanent jobs, beyond normal daily travelling distance.

- **Jobfinder's Grant**. A one-off payment of £200 to encourage long-term unemployed job seekers to consider taking lower-paid permanent jobs. Grants are paid to applicants when they start work, if the job and the job seeker meet with the appropriate eligibility conditions.

- **Work Trials**. A trial period of up to 15 days for an actual vacancy for a permanent position. Applicants will normally have been unemployed for over six months (though some New Deal participants have different eligibility conditions). Benefit is not affected for the duration of the Work Trial.

- **Programme Centres, Jobclubs and Jobplan**. Individually tailored help for long-term unemployed job seekers to help improve their employability and job search techniques. Participants attend local resource centres and undertake selected modules covering topics such as CV preparation and telephone techniques. Other services such as vacancy advertising, use of photocopiers, stamps and telephones are also provided.

Removing barriers in the benefits system

17.   While ONE and the New Deal will provide active support to reconnect people to work, the benefits system itself presents barriers to those with a long-term illness or disability experiencing the world of work. Box 4.3 describes how we have reviewed the rules and introduced reforms to improve work incentives.

Box 4.3: Removing barriers in the benefits system

- The **Welfare Reform and Pensions Bill** will reform the All Work Test in Incapacity Benefit so that, as well as determining entitlement to benefits, it also provides information about people's capabilities which can be used to help them plan a return to work.

- A new **linking rule** for longer-term incapacity benefits which will enable people to take a job secure in the knowledge that if within a 52-week period the job does not work out, they are entitled to claim benefit at the same rate as when they left.

- New rules allow lone parents to remain entitled to Income Support for two weeks when they move into full-time work.

- The **16-hour restriction on the amount of voluntary work** that can be done by people receiving incapacity benefits has been removed.

- The **therapeutic earnings limit** has been significantly increased to align with the National Minimum Wage.

- We are **piloting changes to benefit rules** aimed at helping people with disabilities who want to return to work – initial pilots will allow those on incapacity benefits to earn a small amount of money (up to £15 a week) without losing benefit; and to test out a job for a trial period while remaining on benefit.

- We are **piloting further financial incentives to work**, involving a Job Match payment of £50 a week for those moving into part-time work; and a Jobfinder's Grant of £200 for those starting work.

Box 4.4: Monitoring our progress

Building a proactive welfare system to help people into work

Our priority aim is to help people back into work. We will measure our progress by monitoring the proportion of: people in employment; workless households; and the number of working-age people who have been claiming benefits for a long period of time. We will also be monitoring the employment rates of disadvantaged groups.

Future policy milestones

- Pilots to help people on Incapacity Benefit into work (the £15 disregard and work trials) – **next steps to be announced later this year**.

- New Deals rolled out nationally. New Deal for the Over-50s will have Pathfinders in place from October 1999, **with national roll-out early in 2000**.

- Employment Zones will be fully implemented in **April 2000**.

- Evaluation of Code of Practice for Age Diversity in Employment – **2001**.

Indicators of success

- An increase in the proportion of working-age people in employment, over the economic cycle.

- A reduction in the proportion of working-age people living in workless households, for households of a given size, over the economic cycle.

- A reduction in the number of working-age people living in families claiming Income Support or income-based Jobseeker's Allowance who have been claiming these benefits for long periods of time.

- An increase in the employment rates of disadvantaged groups – people with disabilities, lone parents, ethnic minorities and the over-50s – and a reduction in the difference between their employment rates and the overall rate.

Making work pay

18. People who move from benefits to work – often overcoming significant barriers to do so – should be financially better off as a result. Poor incentives to work have contributed to high levels of structural unemployment and low levels of labour participation. Our strategy depends on people having financial incentives to work. We have a number of radical policies to make sure that work pays.

Radical policies providing financial incentives to work.

- **Working Families' Tax Credit (WFTC)** will be introduced from October 1999. Every family with children and full-time earnings will be guaranteed a minimum income of £10,400 a year, with a generous childcare tax credit also available. By 2001, about 1.5 million working families will be receiving WFTC, around 500,000 more than would have received Family Credit, which it replaces.

- **Disabled Person's Tax Credit (DPTC)** will be introduced from October 1999. It is more generous than the Disability Working Allowance it replaces, with higher earnings thresholds and a reduction in the rate at which it is withdrawn as income increases. DPTC will provide an income guarantee of over £150 a week for a single person with a disability who moves from benefit to full-time work, and £230 for a couple with one child aged under 11 and one earner moving from benefit to full-time work.

- **A new Employment Credit** will be available as part of the New Deal for the Over-50s (in Pathfinders from October 1999 and nationally from early 2000), aimed at tackling low levels of in-work income for those aged over 50 moving off welfare back into work. People over 50 who return to full-time work after six months or more on benefits will be eligible for £60 a week for the first year back in work and £40 a week for part-time work.

- **National Minimum Wage** underpins the reforms to make work pay. Together with tax and benefit reforms, the minimum wage will promote work incentives and ensure greater fairness. It will boost the hourly wage of almost two million low-paid workers – two out of three of them women – by an average of 30 per cent.

- **Reforms of tax and National Insurance** in April 1999 remove labour market distortions and reduce the burden on the low paid. The payment of the Working Families' and Disabled Person's Tax Credits directly through the pay packet will reinforce the link between work and work that pays. And the new 10p rate of income tax will halve the rate of income tax for 1.8 million people, of whom 1.5 million are low paid, and the majority of whom are women.

- **Smoothing the transition into work**. In the 1998 Budget we introduced arrangements whereby lone parents who have received Income Support or income-based Jobseeker's Allowance for six months and who find a job will have their entitlement to benefits protected – at the same rate – for 12 weeks. This will help to give lone parents the confidence to try out a job, safe in the knowledge that if it does not work out, they will not be penalised by the benefits system. In addition, the 1999 Budget introduced a new scheme whereby lone parents returning to work can keep their Income Support for two weeks.

- **Family-friendly employment policies**. As well as introducing a fairer framework of family-friendly employment rights on working hours, part-time working, parental and maternity leave we are planning a campaign to encourage more employers to offer flexible working arrangements to their staff, such as term-time working, help with childcare or dependants, job sharing or shift swapping. These policies will help to reduce the financial penalties of parenthood (and particularly motherhood) and increase the lifelong earnings potential of people who have, in the past, been disadvantaged.

- **National Childcare Strategy**. We aim to ensure good quality, affordable childcare for children aged 0–14 years in every neighbourhood. Further details are described in **Chapter 3**.

19. These policies will help make work pay and reduce the number of people who face very high marginal tax and benefit withdrawal rates. Box 4.5 shows the impact of our reforms on marginal deduction rates.

Box 4.5: Keeping more of what you earn

The combined effect of Budget 99 and the Government's reforms since the election on high marginal tax and benefit withdrawal rates[26] are shown below.

Marginal deduction rates	Before	After
100 per cent or more	5,000	0
90 per cent or more	115,000	15,000
80 per cent or more	255,000	175,000
70 per cent or more	715,000	230,000

Note: Figures are for numbers of families where at least one partner works 16 hours or more, and are based on estimated 1998/99 caseload and take-up rates.

Promoting lifelong learning to ensure people have the skills and education to respond to the modern labour market

20. The acquisition of new skills is a key factor in preventing future poverty and social exclusion: for those out of work it provides access to a wider range of job opportunities and a route back to employment; for those in work, it offers a way of meeting changing job demands, providing greater job security and improving incomes. For everyone, whether in or out of work, lifelong learning promotes active citizenship and improves opportunities to live a fulfilling life. The Green Paper *The Learning Age* (March 1998, Cm 3790) sets out the broad agenda for supporting and promoting lifelong learning in England. The White Paper *Learning to Succeed – a new framework for post-16 learning* (June 1999, Cm 4392) describes our framework for delivering this agenda. Widening access to encourage those who traditionally have been outside the education system are central to this. Specific initiatives include:

- access to free and reliable information about learning – this is particularly important for disadvantaged groups. £6.25 million is being invested in a national learning helpline, **Learning Direct**, which has been established to provide a free impartial service to callers throughout the UK;

- development of **integrated services** involving lifelong learning providers including libraries, further education colleges, schools, and so on;

Access to free and reliable information about learning.

94

- **University for Industry** (UFI) – aims to attract to learning many of the people who are currently deterred, by bringing learning to the home, the workplace and the community. £44 million is being invested in preparation for its launch in 2000;

- **Individual Learning Accounts** (ILAs) – offer individuals the means to manage, plan and invest in their own learning and take charge of their careers and their futures. A number of incentives, including discounts on a range of courses, are provided. Employers and trade unions will also play a role in encouraging employees to open accounts and undertake training;

- development of an **IT infrastructure**, based around the National Grid for Learning and the Public Libraries Information and Communication Technology (ICT) network, which is funded through the National Lottery's New Opportunities fund, providing learners with the widest possible access to free and reliable information about learning. The funding comprises £20 million to train library staff in ICT, £50 million to create digital content for the network and £200 million to help develop network infrastructure; and

- **IT learning centres**, resulting from investment from the Capital Modernisation Fund and the Lottery, are being established across the country and will help all ages to learn or update their IT skills. They will be based in the high street, further education colleges, libraries, schools and other public places.

21. *Opportunity Scotland: a paper on lifelong learning* (September 1998, Cm 4048), sets out the vision and aims for working with partners in education, business, and the voluntary sector for post-16-year-olds' education and skills development. At the heart of the programme is the Scottish University for Industry, due to start operating in 2000, supporting employers and employees who want to learn new ways of creating opportunities for learning for those aged 16 and over.

22. The National Learning Strategy for Wales proposes better access to information through a National Grid for Learning and new measures to increase and widen participation in education. And the Future Skills project, undertaken by a partnership of organisations from the education and local government sectors, identifies and analyses the skills needed in the changing economy of Wales.

23. *Lifelong Learning: A New Learning Culture for All* (February 1999, House of Commons Official Report 1998–99) sets out a 12-point Action Plan for Northern Ireland. This is designed to increase significantly adult participation in vocational education and training; to widen access to the tertiary sector to those previously under-represented.

24. **Higher education**: many people missed out on the chance to benefit from higher education the first time round. Anyone who has the ability to benefit from higher education should also be given the opportunity to participate. From September 1999 students on benefits will be eligible to have their fees for part-time studies waived (in Scotland such students have been eligible for fee waiver since September 1998). Loans of at least £500 a year will be available to part-time students on low incomes from 2000/01 onwards, to help with the additional costs arising from their study. Higher education institutions in England and Wales have also been given a 5 per cent funding premium in respect of full-time students from disadvantaged backgrounds, to reflect the extra support and time needed by them. In Scotland the Disabled Student's Allowance will be provided to part-time higher education students from 1999/2000.

25. **Skills for the over-50s**: many workers aged over 50 have skills that may have been superseded or become rusty, following a period out of the labour force. The *Code of Practice for Age Diversity in Employment* sets the standard for employers to support the training and development of all their employees irrespective of age. National Training Organisations will be formulating age strategies for their sectors.

Gaining appropriate skills needed to find employment

26. A key element of our strategy is making sure that people have the skills they need to compete in a modern labour market. The New Deals aim to provide that. The full-time education and training option in the New Deal for Young People was designed to help young people without existing qualifications at NVQ Level 2 and those with basic skills needs. It offers opportunities to undertake full-time education or training and to enhance job prospects. Participants receive an allowance equal to their previous benefit entitlement while on the option. Education and training opportunities in the New Deal for the Long-term Unemployed aged 25 and over provide opportunities for people to learn new skills or refresh existing ones, in order to help them find or retain employment. And the New Deal for the Over-50s will offer a training subsidy to support the up-skilling of people aged 50 years and over, who have been out of work and on benefits for six months, as they move back into employment.

Lifelong learning to compete in the labour market.

Case study 4.3: Fife Local Enterprise Company

Changing the Focus is a partnership approach to improving the employment opportunities of individuals experiencing long-term unemployment in Fife, providing the opportunity to develop core skills required by local employers. Analysis of the Fife labour market identified a shortfall of skilled workers for the service and manufacturing sectors. Changing the Focus has helped to meet this demand by providing 143 beneficiaries with training and qualifications in IT and Administration. Work placements with local employers give beneficiaries the opportunity to demonstrate their work-readiness and utilise their vocational skills.

At each stage of the programme, beneficiaries are encouraged to direct their own training and learning through a range of support measures such as individual action planning, assessment reviews, guidance and counselling. Fife Adult Guidance and Education Service provides initial support on an outreach basis, working with beneficiaries to develop a career profile.

27. **Work Based Learning for Adults** is a key programme in England for helping long-term unemployed people aged 25 years and over back into work. The budget for 1999/2000 is over £300 million which will provide training for some 120,000 people. About 45 per cent get a job within six months of leaving training; long-term follow-up data show that the labour market benefits of the training provided persist for at least two years. A key element within Work Based Learning for Adults is Basic Employability Training which provides individually tailored programmes to help those who lack the fundamental skills and qualities for employability. Access is limited to those with multiple needs including a lack of motivation, self-confidence, interpersonal and social skills, work habits and disciplines, and poor basic skills. A recent survey of clients showed that about 15 per cent of trainees have never worked and the rest average five-and-a-half years since their last job.

Improving basic skills levels.

28. The **New Futures Fund**, managed by the Enterprise Network and launched in May 1998, is a Scottish initiative to provide intensive support and help for young unemployed people suffering from serious disadvantage in looking for work. The client group includes people from ethnic minorities, people with disabilities and those with learning disabilities who lack basic skills and personal or social skills, those who have been demotivated or are disaffected, those with alcohol or drugs problems, ex-offenders and those who are homeless or with family or relationship problems. The Fund (around £12 million over the next three years) is designed to encourage organisations with experience in dealing with this client group to develop projects that equip these people for the world of work through the provision of intensive help. Fifty-six such projects, involving a wide range of community and voluntary organisations, have been approved so far in the initial six pilot areas. The initiative will be extended to the remainder of Scotland on a phased basis.

Promoting lifelong learning to ensure people have the skills and education to respond to the modern labour market

We want to ensure that all people have the skills to compete in the labour market. We will monitor our progress by looking at the proportion of working-age people with a qualification. Our policy milestones will track our progress in promoting lifelong learning.

Future policy milestones

- Establish University for Industry by **2000**.

- Individual Learning Accounts: establish a national system by **2000**.

- Expand further and higher education to provide for an extra 800,000 people by **2002**.

- Develop a national strategy, following the Moser Report[27] on improving literacy and numeracy, to reduce numbers of adults with poor basic skills.

Indicator of success

- An increase in the proportion of working-age people with a qualification.

Supporting vulnerable groups and those most at risk of discrimination and disadvantage

Reinforcing the rights of marginalised people.

29.   We have set out our plans to help people into work, including policies to ensure they have the skills to compete in the labour market and to make sure that once in work, they are better off. However, we need to go further and to recognise society's responsibility to those who are particularly disadvantaged. We want to ensure all members of society have fair access to a reasonable income and to the opportunities that the rest of society takes for granted. This means intervening to reinforce the rights of marginalised people and bring them opportunities. Society will benefit when all members are able to make an active contribution.

30. We recognise that all people of working age should be provided with opportunities and security. We want:

- to tackle discrimination – whether on the grounds of gender, ethnicity, age, disability status, mental illness or religion. People should have legal protection against discrimination and share the same opportunities experienced by the rest of society;

- all people to have access to high quality public services;

- those who are unable to generate a living income themselves to be supported through a modern and effective welfare system; and

- to provide better support for those on the margins, such as rough sleepers.

Tackling discrimination – improving opportunities for all

31. We must ensure that all our citizens have the opportunity to maximise their potential and to contribute to society. That is the essence of an inclusive society. We intend to promote equality of opportunity so as to unlock the talents of all our people.

People with disabilities

32. We have taken a holistic approach to tackling discrimination against people with disabilities.

Improving access for people with a disability.

- The **Disability Rights Commission**, expected to be in place by April 2000, will help people with a disability secure their rights under the **Disability Discrimination Act** (DDA) and offer advice and support to employers and service providers (for example, shops, leisure services, local authorities and government departments) about their duties under the Act.

- A **Disability Rights Task Force** is looking at securing comprehensive and enforceable civil rights for people with disabilities in the workplace and society more widely. It will report in November 1999.

33. As part of our commitment to civil rights we have been reviewing the operation of the DDA. In December 1998, the Act was amended to bring within its scope employers with 15 19 employees. This means an additional 45,000 employers with 810,000 employees (of whom 70,000 are currently disabled) are now covered by these provisions. In October 1999, the next phase of the Act's access to goods and service provisions will come into force which will require service providers – anyone providing a service to the public – to take reasonable steps to adjust to their policies and practices, to provide auxiliary aids or to provide a service by a reasonable alternative means. We have also begun to exercise powers under the DDA to make transport more accessible – since January 1999 all new trains have been required to be accessible to people with disabilities.

34. From October 1999, the provisions in the Building Regulations dealing with people with disabilities' access to new public buildings will be extended to cover domestic dwellings.

Case study 4.4: Vision Twenty One

Vision Twenty One in Cardiff provides training for people who have learning disabilities. Students can learn ceramic and mosaic skills, workshop practice, and art and craft design in a training programme which is therapeutic and can be a stepping stone to employment. The facilities include a café where students can follow courses in catering, a garden centre where students learn a range of horticultural skills together with general maintenance and retail practices, a workshop for woodworking, a pottery and The Gallery retail outlet.

Women

35. Women are at greater risk of poverty and social exclusion than men. That is why, as soon as we came to power, we set up the Women's Unit to tackle the particular problems faced by women. The Unit has a wide remit and takes a cross-government approach to tackling discrimination against women and unequal opportunities.

36. Key priorities for the Women's Unit are as follows.

- **Women's income over a lifetime** – a project examining the causes of the disparity between men's and women's incomes over a lifetime, which will inform policy development.

- **Teenage girls** – an examination of the reasons why girls' opportunities do not match earlier aspirations.

- **Listening to women** – a national programme of roadshows consulting women about the issues which concern them. We will report on the findings in autumn 1999.

- **Violence against women** – *Living Without Fear* (June 1999, Home Office/Women's Unit) sets out a strategy to tackle violence against women. It pulls together practical examples of good work throughout the UK.

Case study 4.5: Peterborough Women's Centre

The target group for this project, funded by the European Social Fund, is women who want to return to work but lack the skills and confidence to do so. The project aims to secure accurate and consistent sources of advice and resource provision, and to improve access to training and employment opportunities. The project also helps organisations and local groups which give information to women.

The key elements to the success of the project were: a strong and inclusive partnership approach; publishing and distributing findings; the establishment of permanent networks and partnerships between groups; and ensuring that the lessons learnt from the project would be fully explored and made available for other groups to study.

37. In Scotland, research on women's issues in local partnership is being undertaken to examine how best to take gender issues into account.

Ethnic minorities

38. We are committed to promoting equal opportunities for all ethnic groups in our society, and are determined that every individual can maximise his or her potential whatever their ethnic background. We intend to make sure that all sections of the population are properly protected against crime, that we promote equal opportunities in education and employment, and ensure that our institutions properly reflect the ethnic diversity of our society.

Maximising the potential of every individual, whatever their ethnic background.

39. In order to meet these goals, we are taking a number of important steps. We have:

   * introduced new measures to tackle **racially motivated offences**, including an obligation on courts to take account of racial motivation, where that can be established, in setting sentences;

   * published the report of the independent inquiry into the death of **Stephen Lawrence** (February 1999, Cm 4262–I);

   * taken steps to introduce goals – not quotas – for the **recruitment, retention and promotion** of ethnic minorities in the Home Office and the police, fire, immigration, prison and probation services, the Ministry of Defence and Armed Forces; and

   * involved ethnic minority job seekers and businesses in the design and implementation of the **New Deal**.

Age discrimination

40. We are committed to tackling age discrimination in all spheres of life. The Performance and Innovation Unit is pursuing a project on **Active Ageing** (see paragraph 14) – addressing the implications of the trend towards the increasing number of people taking earlier retirement, looking at ways to increase participation in the labour market and the voluntary sector by older people. And it is implementing measures to challenge employment practices that unfairly discriminate against employees on the grounds of age. The *Code of Practice for Age Diversity in Employment*, launched in June 1999, sets out the standard for non-ageist approaches to recruitment, training and development, promotion, redundancy and retirement.

Human Rights Act 1998

41. All UK citizens, including the disadvantaged and vulnerable, deserve legal protection so that they can exercise their rights. We are promoting rights by giving further effect in the UK courts, through the Human Rights Act, to rights and freedoms guaranteed under the European Convention on Human Rights.

Improving public services

42. Our goal is to ensure that all sections of society have fair and equal access to high-quality public services. We are taking steps to achieve that goal.

Access to the best healthcare

43. Poor health can limit people's participation in society, and we know that poverty and social exclusion can have adverse effects on health. That is why we are tackling health inequalities and improving services for all people. Tackling health inequalities is a priority for health and social services. *Saving Lives: Our Healthier Nation* (July 1999, Cm 4386) sets out our strategy to tackle poor health (see Box 4.8). The strategy contains targets in four priority areas: cancer, coronary heart disease and stroke, accidents, and mental health.

Box 4.8: Improving health for all

Saving Lives: Our Healthier Nation is an action plan for tackling poor health and improving the health of everyone in England, especially those worst off.

We will reorientate the NHS to ensure that for the first time ever, health improvement will be integrated into the local delivery of healthcare.

- Health authorities have a new role in improving the health of local people.

- Primary care groups and primary care trusts have new responsibilities for public health.

Local authorities will work in partnership with the NHS to plan for health improvement.

- Health Action Zones (HAZs) will break down barriers in providing services and tackle geographical inequalities in health (see **Chapter 6** for more information on HAZs).

- We have launched Healthy Living Centres funded by £300 million of lottery money through the New Opportunities Fund to promote health initiatives across the UK. The Fund is responsible for developing a network of centres which will target disadvantaged sectors of the population. It will involve the local community in the planning of projects.

- We have introduced local targets for preventing and reducing smoking. In particular, there will be access to services to help people stop smoking, especially for people who are disadvantaged.

Case study 4.6: East London and City Health Action Zone

The East End of London covering the boroughs of Hackney, Newham and Tower Hamlets is a disadvantaged area including high incidence of poor health. The Health Action Zone (HAZ) here is working with local people, together with the private sector to address local health issues. The HAZ will:

- run a **Citizen's Jury on Access to Information** to find out more about how the public view the accessibility and quality of public information currently available;

- fund good quality **translations** for the 40 or more community languages spoken in East London;

- work with co-operative initiatives/pilots to increase access to **low-cost healthy foods**;

- promote participation in the **healthy schools schemes**; and

- examine the potential for the NHS to work with partners from business, the independent sector and others involved in **community regeneration** locally, to tackle the obstacles that inhibit service development in the inner city.

Case study 4.7: West End Healthy Living Centre

This healthy living centre was opened by the Prime Minister in May 1996, in one of the more deprived areas of Newcastle.

This is a project to enable people living and working in the west end of Newcastle to have more control over their health and their quality of life. It is three years old and follows a holistic approach and is a good example of joined-up thinking, services and activities. It has attracted a high level of take-up by local people, mostly on a voluntary basis.

The project provides opportunities which are appropriate and accessible to enable people to make the best of their health and increase their knowledge about health and factors influencing ill-health. A community development project is based at the centre, which undertakes constant health-needs assessment with a wide range of community groups and organisations, responding to recommendations and findings.

Action on mental health

44. We are also targeting mental health. Mental health problems are a key barrier to social inclusion, and are a major cause of poor physical health, disability and mortality. Disadvantaged people are at particular risk of suffering poor mental health; more contemplate suicide and more actually commit suicide than people who are better off[28]. People with mental illness have increased sickness absence, change jobs more often and are more likely to be unemployed. The action we are taking on mental health includes:

    - developing mental health promotion strategies in schools, workplaces and prisons which enhance social support and coping strategies and which tackle bullying;

    - developing **NHS Direct** and its links to specialist mental health helplines, as a source of advice for those in mental distress; and

    - the **National Service Framework for Mental Health** in England and the **Mental Health Services** in Scotland, which will ensure the development of high quality services for those suffering from mental health problems.

45. We have also introduced the **Healthy Workplace Initiative** for people of working age, both in and out of work. It emphasises that the health of people at work is a core issue for both employers and employees. It seeks to encourage better access to health services and provide a bridge between prevention, treatment and rehabilitation. Together with other policies, this will help keep people in work as well as getting them back to work.

46. The White Paper *Towards a Healthier Scotland* (February 1999, Cm 4269) identifies a three-pronged approach based on improving life circumstances, encouraging healthy lifestyles, and addressing major health problems to provide better health for all, recognising that some groups – children and disadvantaged groups – need more help.

47. *Better Health – Better Wales* (May 1998, Cm 3922) and *Well into 2000, a positive agenda for health and well-being* (Department of Health and Social Services, Northern Ireland, 1997) proposes a strategy for reducing health inequalities through collaboration across public services, voluntary and private sectors, and communities.

Access to decent housing

48. A modern housing policy is essential to ensure everyone has the opportunity of a decent home – a key element of social inclusion. The current system of housing and Housing Benefit has weaknesses which we must address. We have already announced our intention to publish a Green Paper on Housing Policy; we want to consult widely on options for reform. We will develop stable and sustainable policies meeting our objectives for housing and welfare reform.

> Mental health problems are a key barrier to social inclusion, and are a major cause of poor physical health, disability and mortality.

49.   We recognise the importance of access to decent housing for people of working age. They can suffer ill health, fewer employment opportunities and other forms of social exclusion if they are living in poor housing conditions or are homeless. And, certain groups – ethnic minorities, lone parents and people with a long-term illness or disability – are all more likely than average to live in poor housing. Our increased investment in housing (described in **Chapter 3**) will lead to a reduction in the number of poor-condition homes for all age groups. We discuss the issue of homelessness in paragraphs 59 to 61 below.

Helping carers and people with a disability

50.   In building the new Welfare State we have emphasised the importance of active intervention to help people get work. The Government recognises that work is not an option for some people, sometimes temporarily and, for a very small group, there is no realistic prospect of them ever earning their own living.

51.   A comprehensive, modern and efficient social security system remains a vital function of a civilised society. We provide a wide range of benefits through the social security system, designed to meet the divergent needs of people who are unable to work because of a long-term illness or disability or those who are carers. Below, we set out how we are providing extra help for people with a long-term illness or disability and how we are improving support for carers.

A comprehensive, modern and efficient social security system.

People with a long-term illness or disability

52.   People with a long-term illness or disability are more likely to be excluded from society. We are making sure that we provide extra support for those people with disabilities who most need it.

53.   The measures we have introduced to help people with disabilities into work are described earlier in this chapter. And **Chapter 3** sets out how we are providing extra help for young people with disabilities and families with disabled children. People with disabilities will also benefit from our proposals for a new State Second Pension which will help them build up additional pension entitlement during periods when they are unable to work. Further details of this new pension are in **Chapter 5**.

54.   As part of our commitment we will introduce the new Disability Income Guarantee in April 2001. This will provide extra help and security for the poorest people with disabilities with the highest care needs. It will provide help through the income-related benefits (Income Support, income-based Jobseeker's Allowance, Housing Benefit and Council Tax Benefit) to severely disabled adults and families with disabled children who get the highest rate care component of Disability Living Allowance.

55.   This extra support will be paid through a new higher rate of disability premium. At April 1998 rates it will be worth an extra £5.75 a week for a single adult or child, and £8.30 a week for a couple.

56.   The Disability Income Guarantee and the State Second Pension, together with the other measures we are taking as part of our welfare reforms, show that we are committed to helping people with disabilities and responding to their needs and concerns with a range of measures which will make a difference to their lives. These measures will provide more help to those who need it most, to enable them to live independently and in dignity.

Box 4.9: An example to show the impact of the Disability Income Guarantee

Under current arrangements

Peter (46) cannot work because he has very severe rheumatoid arthritis which affects arms, shoulders, hips, legs and feet. He needs assistance day and night. This is provided by his wife Joan (43). Peter and Joan receive a total of **£210.40** each week in benefits (at 1998 rates), made up of £19.85 Income Support, £64.70 Incapacity Benefit (long-term rate), £38.70 Invalid Care Allowance (paid to Joan), and £87.15 Disability Living Allowance (highest rates of both care and mobility components). They also get full housing and council tax benefits.

Extra help from April 2001

Following the introduction of the Disability Income Guarantee in 2001, Peter and Joan would receive an extra £8.30 a week, at 1998 benefit rates – the extra amount that they will actually get will depend on how much benefit rates are uprated by 2001. The extra money would be paid as a higher rate of the disability premium, which would rise by £8.30 a week to £38.90 a week. At 1998 benefit levels, they would then receive each week: £28.15 Income Support, £64.70 Incapacity Benefit (long-term rate), £38.70 Invalid Care Allowance (paid to Joan), and £87.15 Disability Living Allowance (highest rates of both care and mobility components). Their total income would be **£218.70** a week, again before full housing and council tax benefits. **Under the Disability Income Guarantee, the couple are £8.30 a week better off.**

Carers

57.   Some six million people are carers in Britain. They are more vulnerable to the problems of social exclusion: they are isolated from the rest of society because their caring duties tie them to their homes and they may face insecurity in old age because their working lives are disrupted. They play a vital role in our society and they deserve recognition for the work they do and better support from the Government.

58.   That is why we have introduced our **National Carers Strategy**. Key elements of the strategy are set out below.

Box 4.10: Key elements of the National Carers Strategy

- Investing £140 million over the next three years to provide grants for carers to enable them to take a break from caring.

- Better information for carers about their rights and the help available to them.

- Better support for carers through involving them in planning and provision of services.

- Help with building better pensions – our Green Paper *A new contract for welfare: PARTNERSHIPS IN PENSIONS* (December 1998, Cm 4179), sets out our proposals for a new State Second Pension which, in time, will help carers build up a pension sufficient to lift them above the Minimum Income Guarantee. By 2040, at least four million people (mainly women) will benefit by up to £49 a week at current rates for a lifetime carer (more details on this new pension are in **Chapter 5**).

Bringing people back from the margins

Rough sleeping

59.   Homelessness, and more specifically rough sleeping, is one of the most extreme manifestations of social exclusion. We are determined to tackle both the problem itself and its causes. Following the Social Exclusion Unit's report *Rough Sleeping* (July 1998, Cm 4008), we have made a commitment to cut the numbers of people sleeping rough by two-thirds by 2002. A Ministerial Committee has been established to ensure effective co-ordination across government of policies to prevent and tackle rough sleeping. Providing housing is only part of the strategy, but we are also taking action to block the paths which lead to homelessness in the first place, including relationship breakdown, poor mental and physical health, drug or alcohol problems, exclusion from school and employment, and lack of preparation for independence for those from institutional backgrounds. For example, the Ministry of Defence is developing more extensive resettlement and support systems for those leaving the Armed Forces and the Home Office is putting in place better support systems for those leaving prison.

Helping rough sleepers back into independent living.

60. We are providing funds to tackle the health, education, training and housing needs of people sleeping rough, with a budget of £145 million over the next three years in London. Elsewhere in England, local authorities are in the lead in tackling rough sleeping in their areas, working in partnership with other bodies. The voluntary sector agencies also have a vital role to play, and we are providing grants for 250 of them across the country for outreach and resettlement services to help rough sleepers back into society and independent living.

61. In Scotland, a wide-ranging review of the causes and nature of homelessness has recently been established. We are investing £30 million over five years, through the **Rough Sleepers Initiative**, to help Scottish local authorities lead partnerships to reduce the numbers of rough sleepers.

Case study 4.8: Examples of the Rough Sleepers Initiative

Edinburgh

Stopover 2 (now called No 20) provides supported accommodation for young women. The **Rough Sleepers Initiative** (RSI) has funded the refurbishment of the building and a team of two full-time and two part-time staff, with a resident warden.

The Homeless Outreach Project, which works mainly with people with mental health problems, received RSI funding for three full-time workers.

Glasgow

Glasgow City Council, Barnardos and the YMCA jointly fund a street outreach team called the City Centre Initiative. RSI funding has paid for additional team members and has allowed the operating hours of the initiative to be increased.

Drugs

62. Misuse of drugs is a very real problem in our society. It limits the ability of the user to participate in day-to-day life, and can cause ill health, and in extreme cases, death. Drugs are a threat to people of all ages and severe problems are faced by some communities because of drug-related crime. Our vision is of an increasingly drug-free society.

63. In our White Paper *Tackling Drugs to Build a Better Britain* (April 1998, Cm 3945) we set out a ten-year programme to rid our society of the cycle of drugs and crime. We have identified four main areas we need to tackle:

- helping young people resist drug misuse in order to achieve their full potential;

- protecting communities from drug-related anti-social and criminal behaviour;

- enabling those with drug problems to overcome them and live healthy lives; and

- stifling the availability of illegal drugs on our streets.

64. In the first annual report following on from the White Paper we set out four challenging new UK targets for 2005 and 2008 (see Box 4.11). *Tackling Drugs in Scotland: Action in Partnership* (March 1999), the report *Forward Together in Wales,* and *The Northern Ireland Drugs Strategy* are building on the four strategic aims outlined in the UK Drugs White Paper.

Box 4.11: UK Anti-Drugs Strategy Performance Targets

- To reduce the proportion of people aged under 25 reporting use of illegal drugs in the last month and previous year substantially, and to reduce the proportion of young people using the drugs which cause the greatest harm, heroin and cocaine, by 25 per cent by 2005 and 50 per cent by 2008.

- To reduce levels of repeat offending among drug-misusing offenders by 25 per cent by 2005 and 50 per cent by 2008.

- To increase the participation of problem drug misusers, including prisoners, in drug treatment programmes which have a positive impact on health and crime, by 66 per cent by 2005 and 100 per cent by 2008.

- To reduce access to all drugs among young people under the age of 25 significantly, and to reduce access to the drugs which cause the greatest harm, particularly heroin and cocaine, by 25 per cent by 2005 and 50 per cent by 2008.

Box 4.12: Monitoring our progress

Supporting vulnerable groups and those most at risk of discrimination and disadvantage

We want to tackle some of the most difficult problems facing people of working age. We will monitor our progress by looking at a range of indicators that capture these aspects.

Future policy milestone

- Implementation of the Disability Income Guarantee – **April 2001.**

Indicators of success

- A reduction in the number of people sleeping rough.
- A reduction in cocaine and heroin use by young people.
- A reduction in adult smoking rates in all social classes.
- A reduction in the death rate from suicide and undetermined injury.

5 Older people

An active role for all older people in our society

In line with other European countries, the United Kingdom is seeing a major increase in the numbers of people over retirement age. People are living longer, and enjoying healthier, more active lives than ever before. For many people retirement is a time of opportunity, fulfilment and contribution to their family and society. But for too many it is a time of financial insecurity, isolation and poor access to services.

Our aim is to extend opportunities for all older people to continue to play an active role in society. Our three key priorities are:

- ensuring that more of tomorrow's pensioners can retire on a decent income;

- tackling the problems of low income and social exclusion among today's pensioners; and

- improving opportunities for older people to live secure, fulfilling and active lives.

Our policies aim to help make people's retirement years as rewarding as possible, and ensure that all older people are given the opportunities they need and deserve.

THE PROBLEM

1. Since 1979, pensioners have, on average, seen their incomes grow faster than any other broad group in the population – their average incomes have risen from well under half average earnings to well over this level[1]. But these improvements have not been shared equally. Incomes of the top fifth of single pensioners have grown by 76 per cent since 1979 (80 per cent for pensioner couples). Pensioners lower down the income distribution have also gained, but by less. Incomes of the bottom fifth of single pensioners – the majority of whom rely on benefits for all or most of their income – have grown by 28 per cent since 1979 (34 per cent for pensioner couples). Pensioners who were unable to save have increasingly been left behind those who have been able to build up healthy second pension and investment incomes.

2. Pensioners have enjoyed other significant improvements in their quality of life. For example, disability-free life expectancy for those aged between 65 and 69 was 13.5 years for men and 15.6 years for women in 1994. This compares with 11.6 years and 14.4 years respectively in 1980[2]. But poorer pensioners have not shared equally in improvements in health[3].

3. To create a fairer society, we need to tackle the causes of these growing inequalities, both for today's poorest pensioners, and for future pensioners. That means adopting a two-pronged strategy – targeting extra help on pensioners who need our help now, and putting in place policies which will ensure that today's working-age population can look forward to a secure retirement.

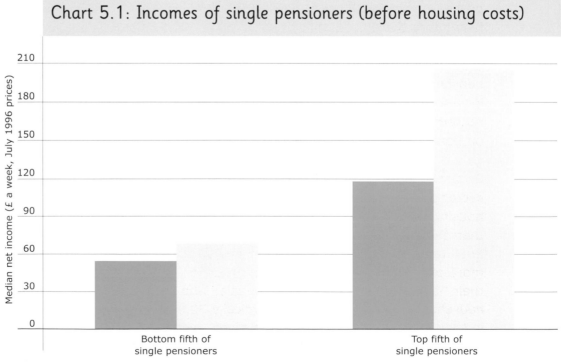

Chart 5.1: Incomes of single pensioners (before housing costs)

1979

1996/7

Median net income (£ a week, July 1996 prices)

Bottom fifth of single pensioners

Top fifth of single pensioners

Position in income distribution of single pensioners

Source: Pensioners' Incomes Series 1996/7.
Note: A single pensioner is a single (non-cohabiting) person over state pension age.

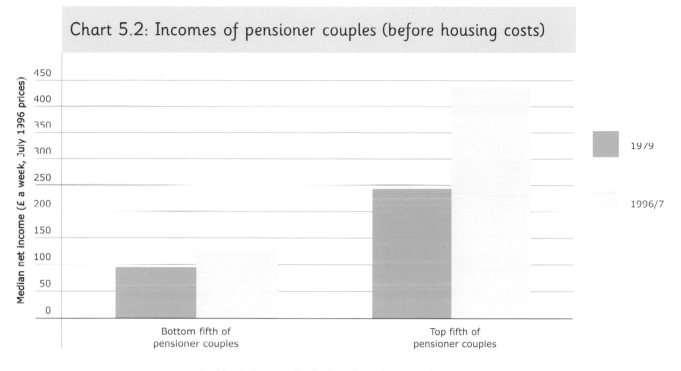

Chart 5.2: Incomes of pensioner couples (before housing costs)

Median net income (£ a week, July 1996 prices)

450
400
350
300
250
200
150
100
50
0

Bottom fifth of pensioner couples

Top fifth of pensioner couples

1979

1996/7

Position in income distribution of pensioner couples

Source: Pensioners' Incomes Series 1996/7.
Note: A pensioner couple is a couple (married or cohabiting) where the man is over state pension age.

Key features of poverty and social exclusion

4.   We have identified four key barriers to social inclusion among older people.

- **Low incomes.** Despite the improvements in pensioner incomes described previously, pensioners are still at disproportionate risk of falling into the bottom half of the income distribution[4]. It is also clear that certain groups of pensioners tend to fare worse than others. Older women make up a disproportionate percentage of the poorest pensioners[5]. And, as the charts below show, the main cause of low incomes in retirement is due to people's inability to save for their retirement during their working lives. As a result they are heavily reliant on benefits for their income in retirement (see Charts 5.3 and 5.4).

- **Poor environment.** Older people, especially those in the private rented sector and those who are very elderly, are more likely to live in poor housing[6]. People aged 75 or over in the private rented sector are more than three times as likely to live in poor housing compared with all people in all tenures. Fuel poverty (where people have to spend 10 per cent or more of their household income in order to achieve adequate heating in their homes) affects many older people, who made up half of all fuel-poor households in England in 1996[7]. Typically 30,000 more people die in winter in the UK than would be expected given average death rates during the year. Those aged 60 and over form the vast majority of the excess winter deaths. This increase in mortality is caused by both exposure to outdoor conditions as well as cold homes, but it is much higher in the UK than in other countries, such as in Scandinavia, where winter outdoor conditions are more severe but homes are more energy efficient.

> Typically 30,000 more people die in winter in the UK than would be expected given average death rates during the year. Those aged 60 and over form the vast majority of the excess winter deaths.

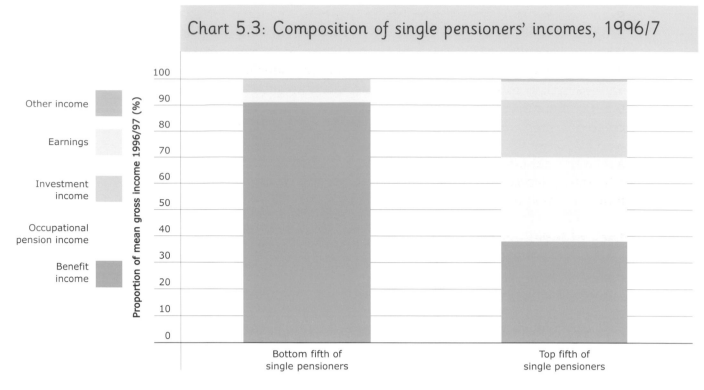

Chart 5.3: Composition of single pensioners' incomes, 1996/7

Proportion of mean gross income 1996/97 (%)

Other income

Earnings

Investment
income

Occupational
pension income

Benefit
income

Bottom fifth of
single pensioners

Top fifth of
single pensioners

Position in income distribution of single pensioners

Source: Pensioners' Incomes Series 1996/7.
Note: Some components make up less than 0.5% of total income. These are treated as zero in this chart.

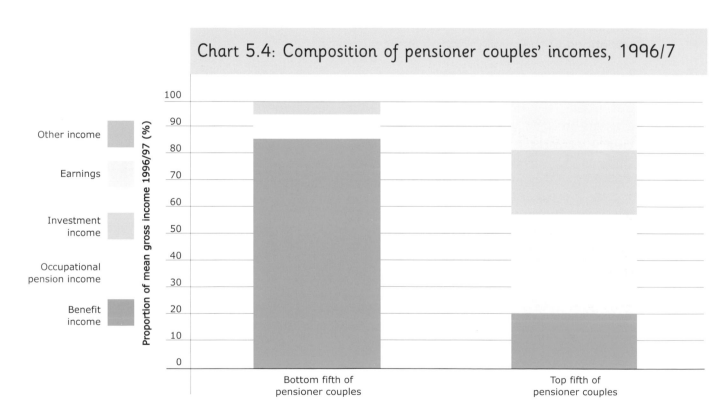

Chart 5.4: Composition of pensioner couples' incomes, 1996/7

Proportion of mean gross income 1996/97 (%)

Other income

Earnings

Investment
income

Occupational
pension income

Benefit
income

Bottom fifth of
pensioner couples

Top fifth of
pensioner couples

Position in income distribution of pensioner couples

Source: Pensioners' Incomes Series 1996/7.
Note: Some components make up less than 0.5% of total income. These are treated as zero in this chart.

- **Poor health.** Maintaining good health is a major concern for older people[8]. Around three out of five people aged 65 and over report a long-standing illness[9]. Analysis of the 1994 Retirement Survey[10] showed that the extent of ill health and disability among pensioners tends to vary according to socio-economic factors such as social class, housing tenure, and educational qualifications. These problems are more common among women[11]. Similarly, the mortality rate for pensioners who had lived in local authority rented accommodation was 16 per cent above the national average[12]; and illnesses such as lung cancer, respiratory disease, coronary heart disease and strokes were all more common among disadvantaged older people.

- **Lack of independence and access to public services**. Older people identify retaining their independence as a key concern[13]. An important element of this is older people's ability to get around safely in their own homes. Older people are particularly at risk of death and disability from accidental falls[14]. Outside the home, older people can find they are constrained from participating in cultural, social and other activities by factors such as fear of crime and poor access to transport. Of those aged over 60, 20 per cent felt very unsafe out at night compared with 9 per cent of younger people; and women's quality of life is particularly badly affected[15]. In addition, older people are more dependent on public services, so if services such as transport are poor, it is older people who are particularly affected. In the White Paper *Modernising Social Services* (November 1998, Cm 4169) we acknowledged that many older people and other vulnerable adults feel the care system is not fair. There are variations in the availability of service, inconsistencies in the types of provision available in different parts of the country, and differences in charging.

The problem with the pensions system

5.   To ensure all pensioners have opportunities to enjoy an active and fulfilling retirement, a decent income is essential. That means making sure that people have the opportunity to save for retirement during their working lives. But key sections of the population are at particular risk of being excluded from the pensions system, because it has not catered for their particular needs. The present system is failing two groups.

- **Those who cannot save** – people who earn less than £3,400 a year do not pay National Insurance contributions and therefore do not accrue directly rights to even the basic state pension – they are likely to end up needing more support from the State. This group includes people who work only a small number of hours, and those on very low hourly rates of pay. In addition those with earnings between £3,400 and £9,000 cannot normally save enough to make a privately funded pension worthwhile (because of the relatively high administrative costs). Due to their low earnings they will receive limited benefits from the State Earnings Related Pension Scheme (SERPS), so unless they are members of an occupational scheme, they will not be able to build up an adequate second pension.

- **Some who can save** – the pensions infrastructure sometimes lets this group down. For those with moderate earnings, who do not have access to occupational pensions, there is a significant gap in the pensions options available to them. Personal pension schemes have not always met the needs of individuals, especially those who have low or intermittent earnings or whose financial situation does not allow them to make the regular contributions required. Too many people lack information about the pension they can expect on retirement and what they need to do to improve their position. And many people simply do not trust the pensions market and are deterred from saving.

6. Women are particularly disadvantaged for a variety of reasons.

- There are around 1.5 million women in work whose earnings are below the Lower Earnings Limit (£3,400)[16] – they are not directly accruing pension rights.

- Women with personal pensions, on average, have lower earnings than men[17], and are therefore likely to make smaller contributions leading to lower future pensions.

- Women are more likely than men to play caring roles, and are therefore more likely to have breaks from the labour market.

7. In total, only 28 per cent of women over the age of 60, who receive any basic state pension, receive a full basic pension in their own right[18].

WHAT WE ARE DOING – OUR POLICY PRIORITIES

8. The Prime Minister has set up an **Inter-Ministerial Group on Older People**. The aims of the Group are to ensure that the needs of older people are better understood and that action to help them is more effectively co-ordinated across government. The aim is to avoid unnecessary duplication in formulating policies and to ensure that account is taken of older people's needs in developing policy.

9. Members of the Group are taking part in a series of 'listening to older people' events, which are being organised with non-government organisations as part of the UK programme for the UN Year of Older Persons. Ten events are taking place across the UK between May and November 1999. The events include as broad a range of older people as possible and aim to reach out to those whose views are not often heard. The outcomes of these and other initiatives will continue to be a valuable source of information for our strategy of tackling poverty and social exclusion among older people. We have, at this stage, identified three key priorities for action.

- Ensuring that more of **tomorrow's** pensioners can retire on a decent income.

- Tackling the problems of low income and social exclusion among **today's** pensioners.

- Improving opportunities for older people to live secure, fulfilling and active lives.

Ensuring that more of tomorrow's pensioners can retire on a decent income

10. We are committed to tackling the longer-term issues so that more of **tomorrow's** pensioners can enjoy incomes in retirement above anything that benefits could ever reasonably provide.

11. That means making sure that today's workforce is preparing adequately for retirement. The Government and individuals must recognise their reciprocal responsibilities. It is our role to help people who can work to do so, and it is the responsibility of all individuals to take up the opportunities which arise. Likewise, it is our duty to ensure there is a sound pensions infrastructure and it is the responsibility of those who can save for their retirement to do so.

Getting people into work

12. We set out, in **Chapter 4**, what we are doing to help people back into work and to make work pay – the New Deals, ONE, the introduction of the Working Families' Tax Credit and the Disabled Person's Tax Credit, and the National Minimum Wage. Helping people back into work will enable more of them to save for their retirement. We have also proposed a series of measures to end age discrimination in the workforce – to make sure older workers are not constrained in their ability to save for their retirement.

Helping people to build up good second pensions

13. At the centre of our pensions reform is the **New Insurance Contract for Pensioners** as set out in our pensions Green Paper *A new contract for welfare: PARTNERSHIP IN PENSIONS* (December 1998, Cm 4179). These are the basic elements:

- the basic state pension will remain as a foundation of retirement income for rich and poor alike. It will not be means-tested. We will raise it at least in line with prices, to retain its real value over time; and

- we need to make sure that pensioners can supplement this basic pension, either through their own savings or through extra help from the social security system (when they have been unable to save), so that **all** pensioners can be secure in the knowledge that they will have a decent income throughout their retirement years. Overleaf we set out our measures to achieve this aim.

Stakeholder pensions

Stakeholder pensions – a better deal for middle earners.

14. Stakeholder pensions will fill an important gap in existing pensions provision. These are a new type of pension which combines the low overheads and high security of occupational pension schemes with the flexibility of the best personal pensions, and will be available to all. They are particularly designed to help those on middle incomes (between roughly £9,000 and £20,000 a year) to start their own pension, though they will benefit those on higher incomes as well.

15. Key features of stakeholder pensions are:

    - **security** – schemes will have to be run in a way that ensures the rights and interests of scheme members are paramount;

Low-cost, flexible pension schemes.

    - **low cost** – costs will be kept down by marketing to groups of potential members and through employers, and by simplifying some of the rules. To reinforce this there will be a limit on the charges people have to pay.

    - **flexibility** – members who cannot contribute for a period or who move jobs will be protected.

16. Up to five million people could benefit from stakeholder pension schemes.

State Second Pensions

17. The current State Earnings Related Pension Scheme is being improved through the introduction of the State Second Pension. Low earners will be given a dramatic boost to their additional pension. Anyone earning under £9,000 but above £3,400 (the current Lower Earnings Limit) will be treated as if they had earned £9,000. This will more than double their additional pension entitlement and so help to lift those on a low income off means-tested benefits in retirement.

Better provision for low earners and for carers.

18. Many people who have caring responsibilities are making an important contribution to society, yet are not able to make adequate provision for their retirement. We promised that we would look at this – the State Second Pension will help those with caring responsibilities. They will also be treated as if they had earned £9,000 in a qualifying year. Subject to a contributions test at the point of retirement (they will have to have actually paid contributions for 10 per cent of their working life), people with a long-term disability who have interrupted work records will be similarly covered.

19. Those people with disabilities who have little or no contact with the labour market during their working life and thus are unable to build up adequate pensions of their own, are specifically catered for by other parts of the benefits system, both above and below state pension age.

20. Anyone who works throughout their working life (including spells as a carer or off work through long-term illness or disability) will, in time, receive a total state pension above the level of the Minimum Income Guarantee which is provided through Income Support. This means that everyone will have a real incentive to save for their retirement, even if they are only able to make small contributions, or if they have periods when they cannot make contributions at all.

Reforms to the private pensions sector

21. Many people who could save under the current pension system are deterred from doing so because they lack confidence in the pensions industry, because of the complexity of the system, or because they have difficulty finding reliable and affordable independent financial advice.

22. To improve this situation we propose:

   - **better regulation** to restore confidence in the system, including a role for the new Financial Services Authority;

   - **better information on schemes**, including the development of telephone information lines;

   - **better information on people's own need to save**, including an annual statement for all those in public and private schemes detailing their current predicted pension, so they can see for themselves if they should save more for retirement; and

   - **wider recognition** of the benefits of occupational pension schemes, and measures to encourage more people to join them.

Pensions sharing on divorce

23. Sharing pensions will allow some couples to achieve a fairer settlement of assets on divorce. This will provide a more secure pension income in retirement for those, particularly women, receiving a share of pensions rights. It will play an important part towards meeting the Government's pension review objectives.

Box 5.1: Examples of the impact of stakeholder pensions and the State Second Pension

Example 1

A woman begins work at the age of 16 in 2002. She earns £180 a week (at 1999 prices) and her wages go up in line with average earnings. She has children when she is aged 25 and 29. From the age of 25 to 34, she stops work to care for her children. At the age of 35, she returns to work part-time on a slightly lower hourly rate, earning £80 a week. At the age of 40, she returns to full-time work, earning £160 a week and continues to work until she retires at the age of 65 in 2051.

Under the current state pension system, she can expect a state pension income of £48 a week. The new State Second Pension will treat anyone caring for a child up to five years old or earning below £180 a week as if they were earning £180 a week. So, under the new scheme she can expect a state pension income of £84 a week – £36 a week more.

Example 2

A man goes to school until the age of 18. He starts work at the age of 19 in 2005 and works for 46 years, retiring at the age of 65. He earns £300 a week and his wages go up in line with average earnings.

Under the current state pension system, he can expect state pension income of £76 a week in 2051. Under the new pensions system, even without making any additional contributions, the stakeholder pension and State Second Pension will provide him with a pension income of £91 a week – £15 a week more.

Ensuring that more of tomorrow's pensioners can retire on a decent income

We will monitor our progress by ensuring that we put in place policies that help people build up entitlement to a decent income in retirement. Our milestones will mark our progress in putting the policy framework in place. Our indicators will monitor our progress in encouraging more people to build up rights to a non-state pension.

Future policy milestones

- Passage of Welfare Reform and Pensions Bill – **Royal Assent due later this year**.

- Implementation of stakeholder pension schemes – **April 2001**.

- Implementation of State Second Pension – **earliest date, April 2002**.

- Start of new annual pension statements – **2002**.

Indicators of success

- An increase in the proportion of working-age people contributing to a non-state pension.

- An increase in the amount contributed to non-state pensions.

- An increase in the proportion of working-age people who have contributed to a non-state pension in at least three years out of the last four.

Tackling the problems of low income and social exclusion among today's pensioners

24. We are determined to tackle the long-term causes of poverty and social exclusion among tomorrow's pensioners. But just as important is protecting today's pensioners, especially the poorest.

Income

25. We are significantly increasing the benefit income of the poorest pensioners – last April, we introduced a new **Minimum Income Guarantee** in Income Support for pensioners. A single pensioner is now entitled to a minimum income of £75 a week, and couples are entitled to at least £116.60. And older or disabled pensioners are entitled to more – up to £82.25 for single people and £125.30 for couples. These increases mean that, from April 1999, a single pensioner is **at least** £160 a year better off compared with the previous Income Support rate.

A single pensioner is at least £160 a year better off compared with the previous Income Support rate.

26. The Minimum Income Guarantee will be increased year-by-year as resources allow. Over the long-term, our aim is that it should rise in line with earnings so that all pensioners can share in the rising prosperity of the nation. This will mean that we can increase the income of the poorest pensioners at a faster rate than by raising the basic state pension, because the extra help will go to those who need it most. We have already committed to increase the level of the Minimum Income Guarantee in line with the increase in earnings in April 2000. This will mean that a single pensioner will be **at least** £240 a year better off from April 2000 compared with pre-April 1999.

27. As well as increasing the rate of the Minimum Income Guarantee well above inflation, we are also examining the case and options for rewarding savers better, through changes to the rules governing the treatment of resources (income and capital). We plan to bring forward proposals within this Parliament.

28. We want to go further than increasing the incomes of the poorest pensioners. We want to modernise the benefit-delivery system so as to reduce the stigma which is sometimes associated with claiming benefits. We are experimenting with better models, making more intelligent use of databases held by central and local government and improving links with the voluntary sector, to help reduce the burden of the means test. We are examining the options for encouraging more pensioners to take up their entitlements.

29. As well as changes aimed at providing extra help to the poorest pensioners, we are also keeping our pledge to protect the basic state pension at least in line with prices. And our Budget measures are taking some 200,000 pensioners out of income tax altogether, so that they can keep more of their income.

Fuel poverty

30. Pensioners can experience fuel poverty[19] for a variety of reasons. The main ones are:

   • difficulties meeting fuel bills, particularly in the winter; and

   • excessive bills due to prices being too high or due to poor housing, including poor insulation.

31. We have introduced a number of new policies to help older people.

Action to help pensioners meet their heaviest fuel bill

32. As well as the increases to the Minimum Income Guarantee described previously, we are providing specific extra help with meeting fuel bills. From winter 1999, over seven and a half million pensioner households will receive a £100 Winter Fuel Payment, increased from £20, to help towards their winter fuel bill. This will cost around £800 million a year for the rest of this Parliament.

Action to reduce other bills

33. We have taken a number of steps to reduce bills.

   - **VAT on domestic fuel** – reduced from 8 per cent to 5 per cent (the lowest level permitted under EU law).

   - **Gas levy** – reduced to zero.

   - **Fuel costs** – cut due to competition and improved regulation.

   - **Help to improve home energy efficiency** – a new Home Energy Efficiency Scheme is investing £300 million in England, Scotland and Wales, to help tackle fuel poverty for vulnerable households (see Box 5.3).

   - **Housing stock** – investing an extra £5 billion over five years to improve housing which, among other improvements, will make homes easier to heat.

34. And we will be introducing new legislation, when Parliamentary time permits, to bring in new energy standards which will require energy supply companies to support energy saving and insulation schemes for their poorer customers. In the meantime we have asked the energy regulator to extend the existing standards until new legislation is introduced.

From winter 1999, over seven and a half million pensioner households will receive a £100 Winter Fuel Payment, increased from £20, to help towards their winter fuel bill.

Box 5.3: Home Energy Efficiency Scheme

The Home Energy Efficiency Scheme (HEES) is the Government's main grant programme to improve the energy efficiency of the homes of those who are vulnerable to having cold homes. It operates in England and Wales with a similar programme in Northern Ireland. Grants are given for home energy efficiency improvements for people in receipt of a qualifying income or disability benefit, or who are aged 60 or over (who qualify for a 25 per cent grant). Current spending on HEES is £75 million per year with additional resources recently announced, in the Comprehensive Spending Review, for energy efficiency of £50 million in 2000/01 and £100 million in 2001/02.

The New Home Energy Efficiency Scheme – a programme for warmer healthier homes

Proposals for an enhanced HEES were published for consultation in May 1999. We propose to provide a package of insulation and/or heating measures for households in receipt of an income-related or disability-based benefit by:

- increasing the maximum HEES grant from £315 to £700, and for those aged over 60, the maximum insulation grant limit will be increased to £1,800;

- increasing the materials-only grant maximum from £160 to £250;

- reducing the costs of heating a three-bedroom detached property by up to £600 a year; and

- providing additional assistance for those aged over 60 living in low-income households, claiming income-related benefits through new HEES Plus.

The devolved administrations will be taking forward their own programmes, but will share the £300 million investment in this scheme. Northern Ireland is funded separately through their Domestic Energy Efficiency Scheme and a review of the scheme will be carried out.

Box 5.4: Healthy Homes Initiative

The Scottish Parliament is committed to improving housing and energy efficiency and has established a joint social inclusion and housing committee. A key policy instrument for addressing these issues is the **Healthy Homes Initiative** which prioritises the needs of the elderly and those on low incomes.

From 1 July 1999 the £12 million **Warm Deal** replaced the HEES in Scotland, offering pensioners who depend on benefits a package of work and advice worth up to £500 to tackle fuel poverty.

Case study 5.1: Sheffield Health Action Zone

Sheffield Health Action Zone is aiming to increase the proportion of older people living in safe, warm, healthy housing through an initiative to strengthen the link between the health, social care and housing sectors. A post is being funded to provide training and support for both housing and primary care staff in order that the health dimension is taken into account when housing needs are assessed.

Box 5.5: Monitoring our progress

Tackling the problems of low income and social exclusion among today's pensioners

We want to ensure that our policies are making a real difference to pensioners' lives. Our policy milestones chart the next steps in raising the incomes of low-income pensioners. Our indicators will track our progress in raising the incomes of the poorest pensioners and increasing their ability to keep their homes warm.

Future policy milestones

- Uprate Minimum Income Guarantee by earnings **April 2000**.

- Bring forward proposals for changes to the treatment of resources (income and capital) for those receiving the Minimum Income Guarantee – **by the end of this Parliament**.

Indicators of success

- A reduction in the proportion of older people with relatively low incomes.

- A reduction in the proportion of older people with low incomes in an absolute sense.

- A reduction in the proportion of older people with persistently low incomes.

- A reduction in the proportion of elderly households experiencing fuel poverty.

Improving opportunities for older people to live secure, fulfilling and active lives

Action on health and care

35. Access to a decent income, and the ability to heat one's home adequately, are fundamental to a decent quality of life. But we also need to improve older people's access to quality health and social care, make sure that they have the option to stay in their own homes and live in decent accommodation, and that they have access to public transport – all prerequisites for living active and fulfilling lives.

36. Many older people are enjoying a longer and healthier retirement than their parents' generation. However, as Sir Donald Acheson identified in his report *Inequalities in Health* (November 1998), there are wide discrepancies in the standard of health between social classes, between different parts of the country, and between men and women and members of some ethnic groups. Narrowing health inequalities is key to our strategies for improving health across the UK.

37. In order to do this, we need an approach which integrates a range of policies to tackle the problems. That means, for example, developing a better interface between health policies and policies on care.

38. The actions we are taking include:

   * **free eye tests** – introduced for all people aged over 60 from April 1999;

   * **improving social services** – the key aims of the White Paper *Modernising Social Services* are to promote independence of users; to provide services more consistently across the country; and to make the system more convenient, straightforward and centred on users and families. In Scotland, *Modernising Community Care – An Action Plan* (October 1998, The Scottish Office) sets out plans to provide better and more timely results for people needing community care, and to involve them at all stages of planning and delivering such care. *Aiming for Excellence – Modernising Social Work Services in Scotland* (March 1999, Cm 4288) contains proposals to strengthen protection of children and vulnerable adults; and to ensure a confident and competent workforce, capable of delivering high quality services which meet people's needs;

   * **extra resources for social services from April 1999** – delivered by local authorities. In England, £3 billion has been allocated over three years. The figure in Scotland is over £300 million, in Northern Ireland over £110 million and in Wales £166 million. The provision includes new grants to help shift the emphasis of social services to promoting independence;

Reducing health inequalities.

Box 5.6: Promoting independence

Among its proposals to promote independence, the 1998 White Paper *Modernising Social Services* includes:

- the extension of direct payment schemes to people aged over 65. Direct payment schemes allow local authorities to offer cash to people eligible for home care, day care or occasional short stays in residential or nursing homes;

- the implementation of Fair Access to Care Services, whereby the Department of Health will issue guidance to social services departments to help them define and apply eligibility criteria for social care more effectively and consistently;

- a partnership grant of £650 million over three years to foster partnership between health and social services to promote independence; and

- a prevention grant of £100 million over three years to develop preventive strategies which provide low-level support to people at risk of losing their independence.

Case study 5.2: Age Well Programme in Sandwell Health Action Zone in the West Midlands

The Age Well programme in Sandwell in the West Midlands was developed in partnership with older people – to ensure that they have an equal voice in actively influencing policy and practice at strategic and local levels within partner organisations. A range of actions is being developed aiming to reduce isolation, increasing participation by older people in organisational decision making, increasing quality of life and reducing accidents by 20 per cent by 2010. The commitment to involving older people extends to those at particular risk of missing out, for example, those who are housebound or disabled. The involvement of black and ethnic minority older people is also a significant theme of the project.

- **clearer standards in health and social services** – the proposed **National Service Framework for Older People** will set national standards of care in the NHS for older people for the first time. It will put in place strategies to support implementation and establish performance measures against which progress within an agreed timescale will be measured. These standards – which are well under way – will be published, their progress monitored and their performance made public. Poor performers will be required to improve, or face intervention. Emerging findings will inform the final framework; this is due to be published in spring 2000. In Scotland, we have set up a National Care Standards Committee to develop national standards in residential and nursing homes and, later, in domiciliary care;

Clearer standards in health and social services.

- **Care charter** – *You and Your Services*, a draft charter to improve services for people needing ongoing care or support, was issued for consultation in May 1999. It sets out a national framework for the development of joint local charters, which for the first time will advise people where they can expect local standards to be set across housing, health and social services. The Government intends to publish *You and Your Services* this year for implementation by authorities by April 2000;

- **funding long-term care** – in the Royal Commission report *With Respect to Old Age: Long-term Care – Rights and Responsibilities* (March 1999, Cm 4192 – Volume II) the Commission examined a range of options for a fair and sustainable system for funding long-term care; and recommends how the cost of care should be divided between the individual and public funds. The Government is giving their detailed report the careful consideration which these complex and important issues merit, and which the Commissioners have called for in their report. We are also considering the comments of various groups in the ongoing debate on the Commission's proposals. We are seeking a long-term solution that is fair to the taxpayer and to the individual;

- **better help for carers** – we published the *National Strategy for Carers* (February 1999, Department of Health). The objective of the strategy is to bring together a range of initiatives designed to address carers' concerns and give them support. Not only do many carers look after older people but many of them are themselves aged over 65; and

- **developing services for older people from ethnic minorities** – the Department of Health has set up a project, working with 12 social service departments and with the help of external consultants, to develop action plans for improving social service provision for older people from ethnic minority communities. Reports setting out lessons learnt will go to all social service departments in England in early 2000.

Improving social service provision for older people from ethnic minority groups.

Housing

39. Older people need warm, comfortable homes, adapted to suit their needs. The White Paper *Modernising Social Services* emphasised the need for new initiatives to promote independence among older people – housing has an important role to play in this.

Promoting independence among older people.

40. We have already set out some of the initiatives we are taking to improve the housing stock, so as to reduce fuel bills and make homes easier to heat. There are a number of other initiatives which will help to reduce the number of older people living in inadequate accommodation. They include:

- **local authority renovation grants** – available to poorer households to help fund major repairs. The grant, which is means-tested, has no upper limit;

- **local authority home-repair assistance** – targeted at the over-60s and other vulnerable groups to help with the cost of home repairs or necessary adaptations. The grant can provide help of up to £2,000 per application, or £4,000 over three years;

- investing £19.8 million in **Home Improvement Agencies** – 184 government-funded bodies nationwide, which provide older people and others with advice and assistance in arranging for home improvements or adaptations, to help them continue living in their own homes;

- **the Home Improvement Trust** – a non-profit-making body which helps arrange home improvement loans for pensioners who are asset-rich, in that they have equity in their homes, but who are income-poor; and

- in Scotland, the Scottish Executive and the Convention of Scottish Local Authorities are working together to implement a **Care and Repair** programme to help elderly and disabled house owners to carry out repairs, improvements and adaptations to their homes.

Helping elderly and disabled house owners to carry out repairs, improvements and adaptations to their homes.

Transport

41.   An adequate transport system is key to enabling older people with opportunities to join in social and other activities and is particularly important for those who live in isolated communities. We are already investing £50 million a year to improve rural bus services, and will be introducing a new minimum standard for local authority concessionary travel schemes for pensioners. This will guarantee half-price fares on buses in return for a yearly pass costing no more than £5. This requires primary legislation which we will bring forward as soon as possible. In Wales, funds have been provided which will allow the scheme to be introduced on a voluntary basis from 1999/2000.

Making transport more accessible.

42.   The Government published a review of voluntary and community transport in Britain, *A Vision for Voluntary Transport* (July 1999, Department of the Environment, Transport and the Regions). The review will help us build a clear picture of the scale and nature of voluntary transport and establish where current policies at central and local level are helping or hindering the work of the voluntary sector – who play a vital role in meeting the needs of disabled and older people.

Tackling crime

43.   The Government is committed to helping people feel safer on the streets and in their homes, by ending the long-term rise in crime through being tougher on crime and deterring repeat offending. We are making it harder for people to commit crimes, and increasing the likelihood that they will be caught, bringing them to justice quickly and handing out the right punishment. We are also investing an additional £1.25 billion over the next three years in the police.

Among the initiatives of our strategy to reduce the levels of crime are:

- a national anti-burglary strategy for two million homes;

- establishing partnership between local councils and the police;

- redesigning town centres, making it more difficult for those attempting criminal offences and investing £170 million to extend CCTV coverage to make streets safer;

- ensuring all schools have programmes to reduce truancy and keep children off the streets and out of trouble; and

- increasing funding for Victim Support.

44.   In Scotland, *Safer Communities Through Partnerships – A Strategy for Action* (1998, The Scottish Home Office Department) is a blueprint for local authorities to take the lead in forming local partnerships with the police and other groups who can help take effective action to improve community safety. And the Crime Reduction programme is addressing the particular concerns of Wales.

Case study 5.3: The SAFE II scheme

The SAFE II scheme, funded by Nottinghamshire County Council, runs alongside the original SAFE project and aims to reduce levels of fear of crime in elderly people and to reduce repeat victimisation among those who have been burgled.

A carpenter is employed by the scheme to fit locks and make other basic security improvements to the homes of elderly people who are either burglary victims or are deemed to be vulnerable.

The findings suggest that SAFE II's success in meeting its objectives is due to the interpersonal skills of the carpenter, the link with police crime prevention experts and the tailoring of the work to provide appropriate hardware for each situation.

Improving opportunities

45.   Key initiatives include:

- improving opportunities for older people to be involved in voluntary work;

- improving access to cultural activities through setting minimum standards for access to buildings such as museums and galleries; and

- introducing free admission for pensioners from April 2000 at the national museums which currently charge.

Volunteering

46. Volunteers make a vital contribution to society. We have recognised the need to create more opportunities for people who give up their valuable time to help others. That is why we set up the Active Community Unit, in January 1999, to encourage people to take up volunteering and to support those already volunteering by raising the profile of the voluntary sector within government and across the whole of society. And in July 1999 we announced a £6.5 million funding package, over the next three years, for voluntary groups across Britain.

Culture and leisure

47. People over the age of 65 are frequent users of libraries and their use of mainstream library services is often higher than other sections of the population. Many libraries have a range of initiatives to overcome restrictions older people may face in their use of mainstream library services. For example, providing services for the housebound, and provision of transport to and from public library buildings.

48. Older people rely heavily on broadcasting services, both TV and radio, as a window on the world and as a source of entertainment, particularly if their mobility is limited. Public sector broadcasters, and the BBC in particular, must produce programming designed to appeal to all sections of the community, including older people. The recent report of the independent review panel, *Future Funding of the BBC* (July 1999, Department for Culture, Media and Sport), considered various issues of particular concern to older people, including the concessionary licences available to those living in sheltered accommodation and the accessibility of services to those with visual or hearing impairment. The review panel examined various options for change, and we will consider their proposals in the light of comments from the public and interested organisations. (The consultation period lasts until 31 October 1999.)

Box 5.7: Monitoring our progress

Improving opportunities for older people to live secure, fulfilling and active lives

We are committed to improving opportunities for older people. We want them to live healthy and fulfilling lives. Our indicators of success will track four main elements of this.

Future policy milestones

- Introduce a National Service Framework, focusing on those parts of the health service particularly important for older people, for publication in **spring 2000**.

- The long-term care charter *You and Your Services*, outlining the services older people can expect from health and social services authorities, will be published in **April 2000**.

- Introducing free admission to museums and galleries for pensioners – **April 2000**.

Indicators of success

- A reduction in the proportion of older people whose lives are affected by fear of crime.

- An increase in healthy life expectancy at the age of 65.

- A reduction in the proportion of households containing at least one person aged 75 or over living in poor housing.

- An increase in the proportion of older people being helped to live independently.

Involving older people in policy development

49. Decent income, healthcare, accommodation and an adequate transport system are prerequisites for living an active and fulfilling life, but they are only the basic building blocks. Pensioners also want choice and independence: they want to feel safe on the streets and in their homes; they want to be able to contribute to society and to their families; and they want access to high-quality public services which meet their needs – in short, they want opportunities to play a full and active part in society.

50.   That is why the Government is consulting older people themselves, and organisations which represent them, so that we can be sure our policies are in tune with what older people actually want and need. The Inter-Ministerial Group on Older People has a central role to play in this.

Box 5.8: Involving older people

We are involving older people in a number of ways.

- The *Building A Better Britain for Older People* document (November 1998) sought views on what the Government has done so far and what else needs to be done. The consultation period ran until the end of April 1999 and the results are being considered.

- The **UN Year of Older Persons (1999)** – the Government hopes this will raise awareness of the important contribution older people can make to their families and their communities, and demonstrate the value of programmes that encourage active ageing and the involvement of older people. To this end the Department of Health is funding a UK Secretariat at Age Concern to organise and co-ordinate an extensive programme of national and local events.

- The **listening to older people events** – organised jointly by the Inter-Ministerial Group on Older People and groups representing older people's interests. They are a key part of the programme for the UN Year of Older Persons. The objectives of the events are to engage more with individuals – not just established groups – to:

  - widen the debate between government and older people beyond the 'traditional' agenda of issues;

  - find ways of empowering older people to speak and be heard for themselves; and

  - test models that could inform the development of a national structure for consultation and involvement. The first event took place in May, and the programme is ongoing.

- **Research on the attitudes and aspirations of older people** – commissioned by the Inter-Ministerial Group from the Local Government Centre at the University of Warwick. The programme of research consists of a literature review and qualitative research based on focus group discussions and in-depth interviews with older people (aged 50 and over). It is examining older people's attitudes and aspirations, their lifestyles, their relations with local, regional and national government, their views on how they are represented, what older people want and what the Government could do to help. A report of the research will be published.

Programmes to encourage active ageing.

Box 5.8: Involving older people (continued)

- The **Better Government for Older People Programme** will work with local people and local service providers to find out what services older people need and how these can best be provided. The programme started in 1998 and will run until June 2000. It is already focusing on listening and responding to the voices of older people at a local level and stimulating good practice that can be spread through local government. There are 28 local pilots which have been set up across the UK. These will develop and test integrated inter-agency strategies, and examine innovative ways of delivering services to promote better co-ordination and responsiveness to users. The pilots are being led by local authorities, but involve a wide range of partnerships with central government and the voluntary, private and community sectors as well as older people themselves. Well over 300 partner organisations are now involved.

51. The outcome of these initiatives will provide a valuable source to inform future priorities and policy decisions across government, including our strategy for tackling poverty and social exclusion among older people.

Case study 5.4: A Better Government pilot

Stirling Council and Forth Valley Benefits Agency are working in partnership with voluntary organisations and older people themselves on 'Fair Share for Us', a project which aims to make the benefits system more accessible to older people.

The project will create and develop a group of information sharers, who will provide information to older people through their existing networks. The partner agencies will further support the initiative through the provision of publicity material, a Freefone helpline, home visits and information roadshows.

Stirling is one of eight prototypes which are exploring ways to work with the local authority to improve the Benefits Agency's advice and support services for pensioners. The prototypes form part of the Benefit Agency's commitment to the Better Government for Older People programme.

6 Communities

Improving opportunities in the poorest communities

We aim to improve opportunities for all people wherever they live. Over the last two decades the gap between those living in the poorest areas and the rest of the country has grown. Economic and social factors have played a fundamental part in this growing inequality between areas. And past policies have contributed to the widening gap.

Our goal is to bridge the gap between deprived communities and the rest, focusing on:

- reducing worklessness;

- improving health;

- reducing crime; and

- improving educational attainment.

Reinforcing the strong foundations laid out in our national policies (as outlined in previous chapters), our community-based policies target the problems of the most deprived areas. This means:

- targeting help to areas with the greatest problems so we can tackle the root causes of poverty and social exclusion; and

- integrated policies to address the special needs of deprived areas.

This means joining up our approach – building better linkages between government departments, and stronger partnerships with local authorities, businesses, the voluntary sector and people who themselves live in deprived areas. A key element of our strategy will be supporting communities in developing the opportunity to shape a better future for themselves.

THE PROBLEM

1. In the previous three chapters we outlined how we are tackling the causes of poverty and social exclusion that affect the lives of individuals. But one of the most powerful manifestations of poverty and social exclusion occurs when whole communities find themselves trapped outside mainstream society, suffering from a range of interrelated problems like high rates of worklessness; high crime rates; low educational achievement; and poor health.

2. The problems experienced by poor neighbourhoods and communities are complex and a strategic approach is required to overcome them.

Key features of the problems facing the most deprived communities

Unemployment and worklessness

3. One of the biggest problems facing the most deprived communities is the local concentration of worklessness (see Chart 6.1 which shows employment rates across Great Britain).

Unemployment rates are twice as high in the 44 most deprived local authority districts compared with the rest of England.

- In Merseyside, 28 per cent of working-age households were workless compared with 17 per cent of all households in England[1].

- Unemployment rates are twice as high in the 44 most deprived local authority districts compared with the rest of England[2].

- In Easterhouse, Glasgow, the unemployment rate is 12.9 per cent compared with 5.6 per cent in Scotland as a whole[3].

- At neighbourhood level, the concentrations are even higher; 45 per cent of working-age adults in the poorest wards in 1991 were not working, studying or on a government training scheme compared with 24 per cent of the population as a whole[4].

Local residents take only one in four jobs within Belfast inner city areas.

- Extreme concentrations of joblessness can occur in inner cities despite the city overall having a dynamic and growing economy. Research into the London labour market suggests that this arises in part because inner city residents do not have the characteristics, in terms of skills, education and attitudes, to compete in urban labour markets[5].

- Local residents take only one in four jobs within Belfast inner city areas[6].

- Race discrimination is likely to be a factor in the high levels of worklessness in many poor communities.

Chart 6.1: Proportion of working-age population in employment in Great Britain

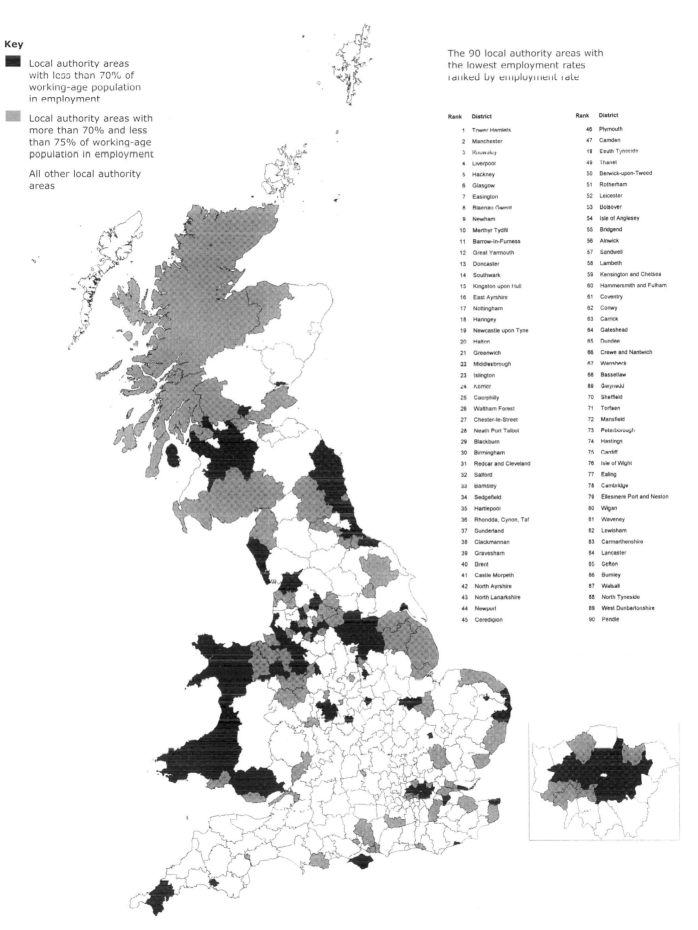

Key

■ Local authority areas with less than 70% of working-age population in employment

▨ Local authority areas with more than 70% and less than 75% of working-age population in employment

All other local authority areas

The 90 local authority areas with the lowest employment rates ranked by employment rate

Rank	District	Rank	District
1	Tower Hamlets	46	Plymouth
2	Manchester	47	Camden
3	Knowsley	48	South Tyneside
4	Liverpool	49	Thanet
5	Hackney	50	Berwick-upon-Tweed
6	Glasgow	51	Rotherham
7	Easington	52	Leicester
8	Blaenau Gwent	53	Bolsover
9	Newham	54	Isle of Anglesey
10	Merthyr Tydfil	55	Bridgend
11	Barrow-in-Furness	56	Alnwick
12	Great Yarmouth	57	Sandwell
13	Doncaster	58	Lambeth
14	Southwark	59	Kensington and Chelsea
15	Kingston upon Hull	60	Hammersmith and Fulham
16	East Ayrshire	61	Coventry
17	Nottingham	62	Conwy
18	Haringey	63	Carrick
19	Newcastle upon Tyne	64	Gateshead
20	Halton	65	Dundee
21	Greenwich	66	Crewe and Nantwich
22	Middlesbrough	67	Wansbeck
23	Islington	68	Bassetlaw
24	Kerrier	69	Gwynedd
25	Caerphilly	70	Sheffield
26	Waltham Forest	71	Torfaen
27	Chester-le-Street	72	Mansfield
28	Neath Port Talbot	73	Peterborough
29	Blackburn	74	Hastings
30	Birmingham	75	Cardiff
31	Redcar and Cleveland	76	Isle of Wight
32	Salford	77	Ealing
33	Barnsley	78	Cambridge
34	Sedgefield	79	Ellesmere Port and Neston
35	Hartlepool	80	Wigan
36	Rhondda, Cynon, Taf	81	Waveney
37	Sunderland	82	Lewisham
38	Clackmannan	83	Carmarthenshire
39	Gravesham	84	Lancaster
40	Brent	85	Sefton
41	Castle Morpeth	86	Burnley
42	North Ayrshire	87	Walsall
43	North Lanarkshire	88	North Tyneside
44	Newport	89	West Dunbartonshire
45	Ceredigion	90	Pendle

Source: Labour Market Trends (Office for National Statistics) June 1999.

4. A much higher proportion of children are growing up in families with no wage earner in these communities.

- Over one in three children grow up in families on Income Support/ Jobseeker's Allowance in the 44 most deprived local authority districts in England, compared with less than a quarter in England as a whole[7].

- Entitlement to free school meals in primary schools in the most disadvantaged areas of Belfast is over twice the Northern Ireland average (59 per cent compared with 27 per cent)[8].

Lack of educational opportunities

5. People in the poorest communities are much more likely to have no or low levels of qualifications and skills. Children's educational achievement is much worse in these areas:

- 37 per cent of 16-year-olds in England have no GCSEs at grades A to C in the 44 most deprived local authority districts, compared with 30 per cent for the rest of England[9]; and

- 37 per cent of the working-age population in Blaenau, Gwent have no formal qualifications, compared with 22 per cent in Wales as a whole[10].

High crime and poor environments

6. The poorest communities are often characterised by high crime rates, poor services, poor housing and a poor physical environment.

- In Scotland, people in the poorest council estates are around twice as likely as those in the more affluent areas to have been the victim of a vehicle or violent crime[11].

- In England, one estimate suggests that as much as 40 per cent of all crime might occur in just 10 per cent of areas[12].

- The most deprived local authority districts in England experience poor housing, vandalism and dereliction two or three times higher than the rest of England[13].

- Over 14 per cent of all ethnic minorities and as many as 40 per cent of Pakistani and Bangladeshi households live in overcrowded conditions, compared with 2 per cent of White households[14].

Poor health

7. People who live in the poorest communities tend to be ill more often and die earlier.

    - Mortality rates are 30 per cent higher in the most deprived local authority districts in England, compared with the rest of England[15].

    - Males and females within the Belfast Urban Area live on average 4.7 and 3.1 years longer respectively than those in the most disadvantaged areas of the city[16].

    - In Scotland in 1996, 11 per cent of babies born to mothers from the most deprived areas were underweight compared with only 6 per cent in the most affluent parts[17].

    - In 1997, around 23 per cent of people in Blaenau, Gwent reported having a long-standing illness or disability, compared with 16 per cent in Wales as a whole[18].

Poor services

8. Typical problems faced by those in the poorest communities are:

    - a poor range of shops;

    - above-average cost for food and other essentials;

    - poor public transport;

    - lack of access to financial services; and

    - lack of access to telephones and information technology.

    Box 6.1 shows the most common characteristics of poorer communities.

- **Poor access to services.** Of 20 unpopular local authority estates in England surveyed in 1994, none had a supermarket or a range of shops, and no more than five had a post office, a GP/clinic, a laundrette or a chemist[19].

- **Inadequate access to competitively priced goods.** One study found that the food in small independent shops, which tend to predominate in poorer areas, can cost up to 60 per cent more than in supermarkets[20].

- **Financial exclusion.** Nearly two million people nationally have no bank account[21]. They tend to be from poorer areas, and have to rely on an informal credit market with all its dangers and costs.

- **Lack of access to insurance services.** 20 per cent of households have no home contents insurance; the majority of them are tenants in deprived areas[22].

High concentrations of disadvantaged young people

9. The poorest areas tend to have high concentrations of young people with poor educational and employment opportunities.

   - In 1996/97, the rate of pregnancy among girls aged 13–15 years in deprived areas in Scotland was nearly twice the rate for Scotland as a whole, and five times the rate in the wealthiest areas[23].

   - In the 44 most deprived local authority districts of England the under-age pregnancy rate is one-and-a-half times that in the rest of England[24].

   - A 1995 survey of secondary schools serving 'difficult to let' estates found one in four children gained no GCSEs, five times the national average, and truancy was four times the average[25].

The concentration of problems

10. All these problems are concentrated in particular areas and act to reinforce each other. It is the combination of a range of different factors that is the defining feature of the poorest communities.

How did we get into this position?

11. The decline in traditional industries, the lower availability of unskilled jobs, and the rise of male and youth unemployment, have had disproportionate effects in some parts of the UK – former coal communities in Wales and shipbuilding areas in Scotland, for example. Changes in family structures have tended to reinforce the economic changes, with more children

living with just one parent. A disproportionate number of lone mothers live in deprived areas with multiple problems, where job opportunities are scarce both for them and for their children's fathers.

12.   Migration patterns have also reinforced economic and social decline. Research has shown that the populations in Britain's major cities have been falling since the turn of the century. Manchester and Newcastle have lost a fifth of their population since 1961. Depopulation has paralleled severe job losses, mainly in manufacturing[26].

13.   The poorest families have been concentrated in neighbourhoods where employment rates are low. Chart 6.2 shows that the social rented sector has increasingly been occupied by households where no one works. As a result, income growth in the social rented sector was significantly less than the growth in incomes overall between 1979 and 1995/96.

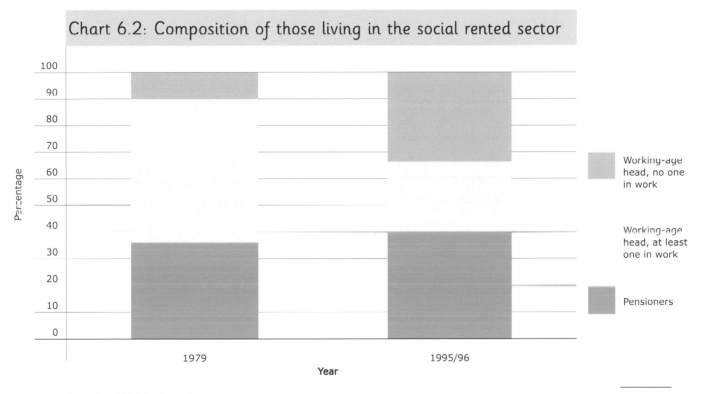

Chart 6.2: Composition of those living in the social rented sector

Source: Households Below Average Income.
Note: Individuals are analysed by economic status of the benefit unit. A benefit unit is either a single person or a couple with any dependent child.

14.   Deprived areas can slide into cycles of decline, reducing the opportunities available to people. As areas become unpopular, those who can move out do so and families with little choice move in. As a result, the area becomes poorer, local job networks disappear and fewer resources in the neighbourhood means that businesses close and services decline. For people who live in these areas, prolonged spells out of work can lead to disaffection and exclusion, and a lack of commitment to the area. This may lead to more crime and vandalism, which leads to further decline[27].

15. In some inner city areas there is virtually no demand for housing. In these areas there are whole streets where most of the properties are empty and even some new and good-quality homes are being demolished. Research has suggested that the gradual breakdown of social stability and poverty, including joblessness, are all factors which are influencing housing choices and encouraging people to abandon once relatively well-occupied areas. Where this occurs it is the most disadvantaged neighbourhoods that suffer the most disproportionate losses[28].

16. High concentrations of workless households in particular areas mean that people are less likely to have any contact with people who are in work, and many job opportunities arise from social contacts[29]. Also, employers may be reluctant to consider applicants from certain areas.

Finding solutions that will bring sustainable improvements.

17. We recognise that local people know best of all about the problems that they face, and that they have an essential role in finding solutions that will work and will bring sustainable improvements. Former policies have not engaged the communities they were meant to help: ideas that are imposed on a community often fail. Our approach is to work with, rather than on behalf of, local people in partnership with voluntary bodies, local authorities and businesses.

18. Problems have fallen through the cracks between Whitehall departments, or between central and local government provision. There are clear links between poor educational attainment, lack of jobs, low incomes and poor services. We need policies which reflect this, but in the past, well-meaning policies have often not tackled the problems in a coherent way. And at the neighbourhood level, there has been no one in charge of pulling everything together. In contrast, we recognise the need for an integrated approach to building better communities with joined-up public services.

WHAT WE ARE DOING – OUR POLICY PRIORITIES

19. The problems are deep-rooted and cannot be tackled overnight. We want everyone to have the best possible chances in life – no matter where they live. To this end, Scotland, Wales and Northern Ireland are developing their own strategies to regenerate deprived communities and promote social inclusion. And, in England, the Social Exclusion Unit is drawing up a **national strategy for neighbourhood renewal** – a comprehensive response to the problems of deprived neighbourhoods. As well as the mainstream policies described in previous chapters, we have two priorities that build on the reform of local government and the review of regional structures and the national strategy being developed by the Social Exclusion Unit.

- Targeting help to areas with the greatest problems so we can tackle the root causes of poverty and social exclusion.

- Integrated policies to address the special needs of deprived areas.

20. We are also currently consulting on future priorities for the European Social Fund in Great Britain – £3 billion will be made available to the areas in most need. This EU instrument provides substantial support for a range of our policies to combat unemployment, develop human resources; and promote employment and social and economic cohesion.

Targeting help to areas with the greatest problems so we can tackle the root causes of poverty and social exclusion

21. Our national level policies to combat the root causes of poverty and social exclusion should make a real impact on the lives of people living in the poorest areas. We know that they are not enough to tackle the complex and linked problems of deprived communities. So, we are also introducing new area-based programmes aimed at regenerating these communities and improving the quality of life for those living in them. Three key themes are central to our approach:

- **the involvement of local people and community organisations.** This is central to the development of strategies for renewal. Local people, local businesses, community and voluntary organisations, local authorities and public agencies need to work together to deliver real and sustainable improvements in each area;

- **flexibility and innovation** – focusing on what works for each community, their particular characteristics and needs; and

- **integration** – making sure that programmes work together to tackle the multiple problems faced by the poorest communities.

22. Examples of organisations working in partnership to tackle inequalities and regenerate their community are shown overleaf.

Case study 6.1: The Glasgow Alliance

The Glasgow Alliance is a multi-agency partnership established to take forward regeneration in the city. The partners include Glasgow City Council, Glasgow Development Agency, Scottish Homes, Greater Glasgow Health Board, the Scottish Executive, the private sector and the voluntary sector.

The Alliance has developed a forward-looking strategy for the city, working within existing resource commitments, aiming to:

- set a context for the city;
- set out the partners' vision for the city; and
- incorporate a range of objectives which all partners will work towards and to set out clearly the actions which each partner will take to ensure that the objectives are achieved.

The priorities in the strategy – launched in May 1999 – include:

- jobs for Glasgow people;
- education, training and lifelong learning;
- housing, neighbourhoods and the environment;
- health and well-being; and
- creating a successful and dynamic city.

The Alliance also oversees the local regeneration activity in its eight priority areas of Easterhouse, the East End, Glasgow North, Castlemilk, Pollok, Govan, the Gorbals and Drumchapel.

> ## Case study 6.2: St Matthew's multi-agency project in Leicester
>
> St Matthew's is an inner city estate of 4,500 people, situated in the centre of Leicester and surrounded by busy commuter routes into the city. Housing consists of tower blocks and maisonettes. It has the largest turnover of residents in Leicestershire; there is a high number of people temporarily resident from Montserrat and, more recently, Somalia. St Matthew's Estate is a core part of the urban regeneration in Leicester, aiming to stimulate economic and employment prospects for the locality. It is also situated in the Leicester Health Action Zone.
>
> Partnership is key to the project: statutory and voluntary agencies are working in partnership to reduce disadvantage. The project focuses on the heart of the community – the Tenants' Association – and emphasises the importance of St Matthew's Area Forum which comprises representatives of all local agencies. The Forum is charged with developing multi-agency solutions to local problems; residents take the lead in developing solutions to meet their needs.
>
> The project is based in Prince Philip House. The site houses the Primary Health Team, the local police office, Drug and Alcohol Services, Community Mental Health Services, Community Paediatric Services and an optometrist.

Regenerating the poorest areas

23. In England, the **New Deal for Communities** (NDC) is the centrepiece of the new approach to tackling the problems of the poorest neighbourhoods. Involving communities themselves is key to delivering sustainable change   under NDC the community will form part of the regeneration partnership, and will be fully involved in the planning and implementation of projects. The key to the NDC is that it will be very flexible and focused on the particular needs of each area. It aims to tackle deprivation in the very poorest communities, and to offer people the opportunity of real and lasting change by:

    - improving job prospects;

    - tackling high levels of crime;

    - improving educational achievement;

    - reducing poor health;

    - making a long-term difference in all of these areas; and

    - focusing on what works, helping local communities develop evidence-based strategies drawing on the best practices of the most successful previous projects.

Improving the quality of life for the poorest communities.

24. Over £800 million will be available, through NDC, over the next three years. The aim is to regenerate the most deprived areas through improving job prospects, reducing crime, improving educational attainment and reducing poor health. The initiative will be piloted in 17 of England's poorest areas, as a test-bed for the principles of a national strategy for regeneration.

25. Alongside NDC, the **Single Regeneration Budget** (SRB) supports regeneration initiatives in England carried out by local partnerships. Over 600 schemes are currently supported, with more than £2.4 billion funding over three years. The scheme has been substantially revamped to concentrate the help it provides on areas of greatest need, including those in rural and former coalfield areas. By the end of this Parliament, at least one major regeneration programme will have been introduced in each of the 50 most deprived local authority districts.

26. These regeneration activities need to be co-ordinated. The new **Regional Development Agencies** (RDAs) are drawing up regional economic strategies to identify regional priorities, and to test out different ways of improving local co-ordination. The Local Government Association has recently launched a **New Commitment to Regeneration**, involving 22 Pathfinder Authorities, all of whom are developing comprehensive grassroots strategies for their areas.

27. We are also providing financial support for business in those areas of the country most in need of regeneration. The RDAs and the Small Business Service will play a vital role in improving competitiveness and creating employment.

28. Effective engagement of, and action by, local people is essential if regeneration activities are to be sustainable. Many local groups lack experience in attracting funding or in managing regeneration projects successfully so we have recently introduced a Community Champions Fund in England to help hard pressed local groups develop these skills. Community capacity-building is also funded through several government departments and the Active Community Unit which works with a range of partners to strengthen the infrastructure of the voluntary sector.

Regeneration in Wales

29. The Welsh Office document *Pathway to Prosperity* (1998), sets out a new economic agenda for Wales. This is an agenda which aims to increase the prosperity of Wales as a whole, and to address the regeneration needs of the poorest parts of the country.

30. The **People in Communities** programme, a key part of the strategy for regional regeneration, includes encouraging healthy living and improving educational attendance and achievement. The programme will operate in up to ten communities in Wales, representing a mix of geographical and cultural settings. Involvement of the community, business and voluntary sectors in effective partnerships working with the new Assembly, central and local government will be crucial to the success of the programmes.

Creating a healthy environment for small enterprises and community businesses to flourish.

31. The **Capital Challenge Fund** provides support for local regeneration strategies, such as the North Wales Slate Valleys initiative, which aims to reverse the trend of migration, by creating an environment in which small enterprises and community businesses can flourish.

Regeneration in Scotland

32. **Social Inclusion Partnerships** (SIPs) have been established to take forward the regeneration of the poorest communities. These partnerships are working at grassroots level on combating the problems of poor housing, ill-health and low educational achievement. SIPs will be supported by £48 million over the next three years.

33. Partnership is the watchword of the new **Working for Communities** programme, which brings together service providers and excluded communities to deliver local services. This will support 13 Pathfinder projects designed to test out new ways of giving local communities more influence over the delivery of local services, and to encourage better integration of local authority and agency working. The programme will allow best practice to be developed and rolled forward to other areas.

Testing out ways to give communities more influence over local service delivery.

34. If the partnership is to work, we need to make sure that the local community has a sense of ownership of the policies. That is why £3 million has been allocated, over the next three years, to the new **Listening to Communities** initiative. It will develop the potential of local communities to participate in decision-making processes that affect their lives, and identify new ways of examining community needs, aspirations and opinions.

Making partnerships stronger.

Case study 6.3: The Fife Community Benefits Pathfinder

This project aims to co-ordinate inter-agency, anti-poverty initiatives in deprived rural and urban parts of Fife. It brings service providers together in small local partnerships, and develops community involvement through the existing community councils and neighbourhood networks to maximise service uptake and reduce individual debt.

Regeneration in Northern Ireland

35. Our **New TSN** (New Targeting Social Need, described in Box 2.3) builds on the original Targeting Social Need initiative launched in 1991 in response to research showing significant differences between the Catholic and Protestant communities on a number of socio-economic indicators. New TSN has a particular focus on tackling the problems of unemployment and increasing employability. It ensures resources are targeted towards those most in need, irrespective of community background.

36. Innovative urban regeneration initiatives such as **Making Belfast Work** and the **Londonderry Regeneration Initiative** have played important roles in tackling the problems of disadvantaged communities for many years. These initiatives are being reviewed to ensure that the most effective response is being made to the needs of the most deprived neighbourhoods across Northern Ireland. There has also been a concentrated effort to improve the housing stock and this has had significant impact for disadvantaged people and communities.

37. **District Partnerships** is an example of this approach. These were formed to deliver projects under the **European Unit Special Support Programme for Peace and Reconciliation**. They involve giving local people the resources and support to identify and address local problems. District Partnerships is made up of local representatives, the community and voluntary sectors and social partners, which allows them to plan strategically in their areas and to co-ordinate multiple activities and funding.

Improving opportunities and quality of life in the poorest areas

An integrated approach to tackling the problems in deprived neighbourhoods.

38. Regeneration programmes, like the **New Deal for Communities**, take an integrated approach to tackling the whole range of problems which occur in deprived neighbourhoods. But some neighbourhoods have particular needs in policy areas such as health, education or employment. That is why we have set in place Health Action, Education Action and Employment Zones to address the problems in an integrated way on an area-by-area basis. Many zones will cover the same geographical areas and where they do we will ensure that they complement rather than duplicate one another and make sure that they learn from each other and make best use of resources.

- We have set up **Employment Zones** to improve employment opportunities for the long-term unemployed in the poorest areas. They will be fully implemented in April 2000 and will offer long-term unemployed people aged 25 and over help to find work, which will include the opportunity of starting their own businesses, by providing grants for equipment, and support during test trading. The Employment Zone will also match those wishing to become self-employed with existing small business people who will be able to offer advice and encouragement.

North West Wales is the biggest Employment Zone, spanning some 100 square miles of spectacular countryside. Unlike other Zones it has no large conurbation so it has to find individual solutions to the problems of a scattered population.

One client who had been unemployed for over four years was helped back into work after a period of ill-health. His Construction Industry Training Board (CITB) licence had lapsed and he was unable to renew it as he could not afford the fee. The Zone's 'Barriers to Employment' scheme was used to fund the re-sit test and within six weeks he was back at work. Over 120 people have found work through this Zone.

- **Education Action Zones** are being targeted on poorest areas to combat the problems of failing schools. We aim to ensure that all children have the opportunity of a good education, so that they can compete in the job market when they leave school (more detail is given in **Chapter 3**).

- **Health Action Zones** are seven-year programmes between the NHS, local authorities, the voluntary and private sectors, and community groups. Health Action Zones (HAZs) are developing and implementing joint strategies to tackle inequalities in the most needy areas, and will deliver measurable improvements in public health and in the outcomes and quality of treatment and care. Twenty-six zones have been set up, covering over 13 million people in England. Their work programmes represent a new approach to public health, linking health, regeneration, employment, education and housing initiatives to respond to the needs of vulnerable groups and deprived communities. We are making available over £290 million to assist HAZs over the period to March 2002.

Case study 6.5: Health Action Zones: Lambeth, Southwark and Lewisham

The Lambeth, Southwark and Lewisham Health Action Zone focuses on 'Children First'. The HAZ's mission is:

"To use the opportunities presented by HAZ to improve the future for children and young people by promoting health, improving services and building strong partnerships."

The core programme is centred around:

- working with excluded children and young people;
- improving parenting skills;
- working with young people who are looked after;
- pregnant girls;
- hard-to-reach adolescents; and
- reducing youth crime.

39. We are aiming to improve the quality of life for those living in the poorest areas by:

New measures to tackle racially motivated crime and anti-social behaviour.

- **tackling crime**. Communities need to feel safe and secure. Local and police authorities are working in partnership with local organisations and consulting widely with local communities in order to make sure we put policies into effect in a way which works. We have new measures to tackle racially motivated crime and anti-social behaviour and to protect witnesses from intimidation;

- ensuring poorer areas enjoy the benefits of the information revolution. The Performance and Innovation Unit's project **Access to e-commerce** is proposing mechanisms to co-ordinate and monitor the variety of Government initiatives, such as **IT for All** and the **IT Learning Centres**, making them available for all groups and to ensure that resources are not duplicated and directed to the most effective projects;

- investing £5 billion over the lifetime of the Parliament **in housing** through the release of council house capital receipts.

- working to improve **housing management** and to ensure that tenants are more fully involved in decision-making. Increased tenant involvement is essential to ensure better housing-investment decisions and service delivery, and to tackle social exclusion:

Ensuring greater tenant involvement in decision making.

  - following consultation, we have issued a national framework for **Tenant Participation Compacts**. These will set out the core standards for involving and empowering tenants and the responsibilities of tenants and local authority landlords in establishing local participation arrangements. All local authorities in England will be expected to introduce Compacts from 1 April 2000;

  - in Scotland, a **New Housing Partnership** initiative has been introduced, with £278 million of public money over the next three years. This will help to lever in significant resources from the private sector and will help to promote community ownership of housing and improve the fabric of social housing;

- investing **£1.1 billion in the Housing Action Trust (HAT) programme** to take over and regenerate some of the worst local authority housing estates in England. Six HATs have been set up in the 1990s. The programmes run for between eight and twelve years, during which time they renovate or rebuild properties such as tower blocks, replacing them with low-rise flats. HATs are also responsible for carrying out extensive social and environmental programmes to ensure that tenants of the new properties will sustain an improved quality of life. These include training and education programmes, help with jobs, childcare, healthcare, financial matters (for example, community credit unions) and programmes to tackle drugs, crime and vandalism on the estates. As part of their strategy, HATs ensure these services can continue after the HAT is wound up – usually by means of tenant-led Community Development Trusts;

- **working with landlord and tenant representatives** and others to develop a protocol for disputes over housing disrepair. This will benefit tenants and landlords by setting out a clear framework for resolving housing disrepair disputes before recourse to the courts. It should be of particular benefit to local authorities and other social housing landlords by enabling them to use more of their budgets for repairs and maintenance on improving living conditions and less on defending court actions;

- developing a network of **healthy living centres**, funded by £300 million of lottery money, to promote health initiatives across the UK (see **Chapter 4**); and

- working to ensure that planning policy improves access to **shops** in local areas and putting in place policies to protect consumers. Those who have low levels of education and skills and the socially excluded can face greater difficulties in assessing the growing amount of consumer information needed to make good consumer choices. The poorest in society are least able to afford the consequences of bad purchases. Our new approach to protecting consumers aims to protect and help the socially excluded.

40. Widening access to justice will also improve quality of life.

- We are **improving access to legal services** – through the development of local networks of good-quality legal services, supported by co-ordinated funding, and based on the real needs and priorities of local people – so that people are better able to find out about their rights and how to enforce them. Local networks will be achieved through setting up **Community Legal Service Partnerships** in every local authority area. The partnerships are currently being pioneered in 49 local authority areas. Some examples of work include specialist debt services, an Internet website to help people find local advice services, and new ways of delivering advice through video-links and GP surgeries.

Improving access to legal services.

- We are **reforming legal aid** to enable us to focus resources on areas of priority need for the less well-off, such as housing, debt, immigration, child protection and welfare benefits, and on cases that raise matters of public interest.

- We are extending and improving **'no-win no-fee' arrangements** to give people on low and middle incomes better access to their rights through the civil courts.

41. A key part of our approach is to encourage and support community self-help. People in poorer areas have traditions of strong community support and in recent years, the old traditions of co-operatives and mutuals have been revived to great effect. For example:

Reviving traditions of co-operatives and mutuals.

- food co-operatives are bringing cheaper and more varied ranges of foods including fruit and vegetables to local people;

- bulk buying through food co-operatives is a good way to reduce the cost of basic goods; and

- credit unions dramatically reduce dependence on loan sharks. **Local Exchange Trading Schemes (LETS)** enable local people to improve their quality of life by exchanging time and skills.

Case study 6.6: Community self-help in Longley

The Longley Community Store is a community-owned and run local convenience store on the Longley Estate in Sheffield which aims to combat the problem of 'food deserts' in poor neighbourhoods and provide the local community with a competitively priced, easily accessible grocery store.

The store, which is a pilot project of the Community Owned Retailing Project (COR), was set up and is run by the Longley Organised Community Association Ltd, an organisation formed out of the former tenants' and residents' groups on the estate. The Association borrowed £25,000 to buy an old furniture shop and COR gave them a £70,000 interest-free loan to refit and restock it.

At the moment, Longley Community Store is trading at £700 a day and breaking even. But, the Store is not yet open full hours, the staff are still undergoing training and it has yet to develop services such as home delivery and newspaper rounds. In time, the store is expected to make an annual profit of £25,000, all of which will be reinvested in the local community to fund community-owned facilities such as youth clubs and children's play areas.

Improving the quality of life in urban areas ...

42. Many poorer communities are located within urban areas. Our White Paper on Urban Policy will set out a coherent government strategy to tackle urban issues in England. It will describe policies to improve quality of life in our towns and cities. We are looking at the combined effect of a wide range of issues, with the aim of enabling communities in our towns and cities to prosper, and to tackle social exclusion.

... and in rural areas

43. Poverty and social exclusion are significant and persistent problems in rural areas, but are concentrated in smaller pockets often with the rural poor closely intermingled with the better off.

44. We have already achieved much for rural areas including:

- an additional £50 million a year for **rural transport** in England;

- the new **Countryside Agency**, with responsibility for advising the Government and taking action relating to the environmental, economic and social well-being of the English countryside;

- in **coalfield areas**, we are investing an additional £354 million in regeneration, in response to the recommendations of the Coalfields Task Force;

- in Wales, the **Rural Partnership** is producing a statement for consideration by the National Assembly. It aims to identify policy and practice capable of delivering substantial benefits to rural Wales;

- in Scotland, additional funding of £3.5 million announced in the 1998 budget is being targeted to improve transport for people living in rural areas. And **The Initiative at the Edge** aims to help some of Scotland's most remote and fragile rural communities; and

- In Northern Ireland, a partnership approach has been key to the **Rural Development Programme** (1994–99) in the revitalisation of disadvantaged rural areas. Various partnerships have been formed:

  - at community level to develop and implement rural regeneration plans or projects;

  - through Area Based Strategy Action Groups, made up of people from local communities, local authorities, statutory bodies and the private sector, to provide local ownership of the processes of consultation, decision-making, implementation of strategy and management; and

  - umbrella groups or networks of groups pursuing common objectives.

45.   However, there is still much to do. Box 6.2 sets out some of the problems which persist.

Box 6.2: Particular problems of rural areas

The nature of poverty and social exclusion in rural areas is different to that experienced elsewhere – access to a wide range of services is much more limited and access to transport is much more important.

The Rural Development Commission's *1997 Survey of Rural Services* found that 42 per cent of rural parishes had no shop, 43 per cent had no post office, 49 per cent had no school and 83 per cent had no GP. In addition, 22 per cent of rural parishes had no bus service at all, and only 66 per cent of rural parishes had a bus service running at least five days a week.

While for those fully mobile the lack of services may not be a problem, those who have mobility problems, face real barriers to participation in society. Transport is a key source of exclusion in rural areas. The population is widely dispersed and often needs to travel significant distances – to nearby villages or the closest town – to access basic services such as shops and work, access to education or training and other forms of social integration. For the 22 per cent of rural households who have no car, public transport is the only way of accessing these services.

46.   That is why, in tandem with the Urban White Paper, we will publish
       a Rural White Paper setting out how new policies will be tailored and
       integrated to reflect rural concerns and improve the quality of life in
       these areas. The Rural White Paper will consider how development and
       regeneration policies can assist deprived rural communities and give
       rural people improved opportunities.

47.   The vitality of rural economies is central to the overall health and welfare
       of rural areas and to the quality of life experienced by its inhabitants and
       visitors. The Performance and Innovation Unit's project on rural economies
       will produce a strategy for delivering the Government's objective to
       facilitate dynamic and competitive rural economies. This will address rural
       exclusion by improving the quality and quantity of employment in rural
       areas. This economic dynamism needs to be sustainable and the strategy
       will also address issues of service provision and access. The Rural White
       Paper will then take this strategy forward.

Integrated policies to address the special needs of deprived areas

48.   The combination of new national policies (outlined in earlier chapters) and
       the new area-based programmes (outlined above) will provide a firm basis
       for tackling the root causes of poverty and social exclusion in the poorest
       areas. There are however some important gaps where policy and
       co-ordination need to be improved. The third strand of the Social Exclusion
       Unit's (SEU) national strategy for neighbourhood renewal is a fast-track
       cost-effective policy development process to fill in these gaps. The SEU's
       report on deprived neighbourhoods set in train an intensive programme of
       policy development. This involves 18 cross-cutting Policy Action Teams
       (drawn from ten Whitehall Departments) with more than 200 experts
       outside Government and many with experience of poor neighbourhoods.
       It is based around five themes.

Getting people into work

49.   The most striking feature of poor neighbourhoods is the high concentration
       of households with no one in work. Three policy action teams are looking
       at the specific problems that face people in these communities, especially
       when they have been out of the labour market for very long periods of
       time. They are addressing the problems of people in deprived areas
       finding work, acquiring skills and setting up businesses. The teams will
       draw up action plans to:

- reduce the difference between levels of worklessness in poor
  neighbourhoods and the national average, and within that to reduce
  the disproportionate unemployment rates for people from some
  ethnic minorities;

- assess the number of adults in poor neighbourhoods who lack essential
  employment related and other life skills, and help them to acquire
  them; and

- encourage more successful business start-ups in poor neighbourhoods.

Improving poor neighbourhoods

50.   People in poor neighbourhoods are more likely to experience crime and anti-social behaviour and live in an area of poorly-managed or difficult-to-let housing. Dealing with these problems is crucial if we are to improve the quality of life of people living in these areas and to attract more people back into them. Six action teams are working on improving the quality of the local environment. The teams will draw up cost-effective action plans to:

- identify models of neighbourhood management and promote them;

- bring about local housing management that is more cost-effective in tackling social exclusion, including on-the-spot housing management where appropriate;

- extend the use of neighbourhood warden schemes;

- identify and tackle the problems of unpopular housing where this occurs;

- reduce the incidence of anti-social behaviour and develop a set of measures to drive and measure progress; and

- raise the numbers involved in volunteering and community activity in poor neighbourhoods; increase the viability of community groups and the services they deliver and encourage the growth of informal mutual support.

Case study 6.7: Working with the voluntary sector to tackle social exclusion in communities

Communities That Care (UK) is a charity, established in 1997 on the initiative of, and with funding from, the Joseph Rowntree Foundation. The organisation's purpose is to develop in the UK a number of long-term programmes to tackle social exclusion and promote community safety using 'risk and protection focused prevention'. The initiative targets problem areas that affect the lives of young people and the communities where they live, and includes youth crime, drug misuse (particularly by 15–16-year-olds), school-age pregnancy and school failure.

In Scotland, three projects (Cranhill/Ruchazie and Easterhouse in Glasgow; Gracemount/Southhouse in south Edinburgh, and citywide in Dundee; have been supported by the Government.

The programmes will be locally managed and accountable. They will operate by establishing a working partnership between local people, agencies and organisations in order to achieve sustainable reductions in youth crime, school failure, drug abuse and school-age pregnancy. These pilot projects will be carefully evaluated so that we can share the experiences and benefits with others across Scotland.

Building a better future for young people

51.   Poor neighbourhoods typically contain a high proportion of young people who experience the linked problems of poor health, educational underachievement, truancy, school exclusions, teenage pregnancy and drug problems. Two policy action teams are addressing the specific problems of educational underachievement and disaffected young people. The main goals of these teams are to develop action plans to:

- identify the most cost-effective 'schools plus' approaches to reducing failure at school and using schools as a focus for other community services; and

- identify what needs to be done to develop cost-effective preventive work with disaffected young people in poor neighbourhoods.

52.   **Chapter 3** contains more details of our approach to tackling problems faced by young people making the difficult transition from childhood to adulthood, especially those most vulnerable.

Access to services

53.   As noted above, people living in poor neighbourhoods often lack easy access to shops containing competitively priced, good quality foods or good transport to reach them. Access to financial services can be a problem, where people in poor neighbourhoods are denied access to bank accounts and other services such as home contents insurance. Three action teams are addressing the availability of key services to low-income individuals and areas. Their task is to draw up action plans to:

- increase access to shopping for people in deprived neighbourhoods;

- increase access to financial services for people living in deprived neighbourhoods; and

- increase the availability and take-up of communications and information technology for people living in deprived neighbourhoods.

Making the Government work better

54.   Three action teams have been set up to address weaknesses, such as poor co-ordination in central and local government to tackle connected problems. This will involve developing a better awareness in Whitehall of the impact of policy on the ground and developing good practice. Their tasks are to draw up action plans to:

- identify the skills, experience and support needed in public agencies and local partnerships to ensure that programmes are designed and implemented successfully and achieve the desired outcomes;

- build on local government reform and area-based initiatives to ensure long-term, broad-based local strategies to tackle and prevent social exclusion becoming the norm; and

- identify how to overcome the barriers to obtaining quality, local-area information.

Case study 6.8: Bromley-by-Bow Centre – an integrated approach to the problems of poverty and social exclusion

This Centre, located in one of the most deprived wards in the UK, seeks to turn the downward spiral of deprivation into an upward spiral of opportunity.

Aims of the Centre

- To create opportunities for people to achieve excellence.
- To create a community of individuals able to engage with local issues and bring about their own transformations.
- To create effective social and economic change in Bromley-by-Bow.

The Centre runs many weekly activities. The major projects over the last year were:

- **multicultural outreach** – outreach and support programmes to allow ethnic minority groups to join integrated projects;

- **café** – the Pie in the Sky café – a community café serving reasonably-priced healthy food;

- **care** – arts and health activity for frail, elderly and disabled people;

- **families** – outreach, counselling and support for vulnerable local families;

- **training** – training and work experience opportunities for local people;

- **health** – new approaches to health, linking health professionals with community work;

- **park** – restoring and maintaining the local park; and

- **youth** – art, sport and outdoor activities for local young people.

What happens next?

55. The Policy Action Teams are reporting in three tranches during 1999 (April, July and December). The work is on schedule. Some have already been published. The Social Exclusion Unit is co-ordinating this work, and recommendations made by all the teams will feed into the national strategy for neighbourhood renewal, which will be published for consultation in spring 2000.

56.   The teams are adopting an open approach, consulting widely, particularly with people who live in poor neighbourhoods. They are also giving specific consideration to race and ethnic minority issues relevant to their topic. The Social Exclusion Unit's remit only covers England. Scotland, Northern Ireland and Wales are all doing extensive work to tackle poverty and social exclusion in a way that meets the needs and aspirations of their people. Boxes 2.1–2.3 in **Chapter 2** describe each country's strategy.

Box 6.3: Monitoring our progress

Our goal is to bridge the gap between deprived communities and the rest

The objective we have set ourselves – to end the scourge of neighbourhood deprivation – is a challenging one. The problems of poverty and social exclusion in the poorest neighbourhoods have built up over time – it will take time to resolve them. But, over a 10- to 20-year period, we aim to deliver real change so that the residents of poor areas can have more and better jobs, better schools, better health and improved safety.

Future policy milestones

- New Deal for Communities roll-out.
- Publish Urban and Rural White Papers.
- Publication of a National Strategy for Neighbourhood Renewal by **spring 2000**.
- Launching the Community Legal Service in **2000**.

Indicators of success

These will reflect improved outcomes in four areas: long-term unemployment and worklessness; crime; health; and educational attainment.

- There is considerable work under way to develop indicators to monitor our progress in bridging the gap. This is being taken forward in the Social Exclusion Unit's Policy Action Team on Better Information; the Department of the Environment, Transport and the Regions' review of the Index of Local Deprivation; and in related work in Scotland, Wales and Northern Ireland. We will report on progress in next year's annual report.

7 Conclusion

A good start, but this is only the beginning

1. This first annual report on our strategy to tackle poverty and social exclusion has set out a threefold framework based on:

    *   **tackling the causes** of poverty and social exclusion, not just the symptoms;

    *   creating a **fairer** society in which everyone has the **opportunity** to achieve their full potential; and

    *   **investing** in individuals and communities to equip them to take control of their lives.

2. We have explained how the measures we have already taken are contributing to the strategy, and listed a range of policy milestones and indicators of success against which to monitor our progress.

3. We have already put in place many key building blocks for tackling poverty and social exclusion, through our policies to tackle worklessness, raise standards in education and new policies for areas which have a concentration of deprivation and serious problems of social exclusion. We have started a process of reform of the tax and benefits system which substantially boosts support for families, encourages work, and lays the foundations for a secure income in old age. We are also breaking down organisational and institutional barriers so that we have integrated solutions for linked, complex problems.

4. But this is only the beginning. Tackling the causes of poverty and social exclusion will take time, and results cannot be achieved overnight. Our emphasis on tackling causes, and prevention, means that children are at the heart of our strategy. Our vision is one of a society in which no child is condemned to poverty, a society where all children have access to a decent standard of living and an education which equips them to fulfil their potential. A good start in life is crucial to equipping children for a successful adult life, security for themselves and their own children, and an independent and fulfilling retirement.

5.   These problems have built up over a long period, and it will take time to resolve them. But we are already seeing signs of early progress in some areas.

- Our measures to improve standards in education are beginning to have an effect. The number of exclusions fell by 3 per cent in the last school year and the proportion of 11-year-olds reaching level 4 or above in the Key Stage 2 tests for literacy rose by five percentage points between 1998 and 1999.

- In total, the New Deals have helped over 150,000 people move into jobs and youth unemployment – those who have been unemployed for more than six months – has fallen by 60 per cent.

- The introduction of measures announced in the 1998 and 1999 Budgets to increase support for children in the tax and benefits systems and the National Minimum Wage will mean that the poorest fifth of families with children will be, on average, over £1,000 a year better off.

6.   But it will take time for these and other measures to work through into a real and lasting effect on the enduring problems of poverty and social exclusion which are complicated, and are influenced by a range of wider social and economic factors.

7.   This report represents an initial 'audit' of the extent of the problem, and the measures we have in place to tackle it. Over the coming years we will be monitoring progress towards our vision, and reporting on this, and on key developments and new measures, in subsequent annual reports.

THE NEXT STAGE

8.   We are building on our strong start in the following ways.

Taking forward the next stages of key policy development and implementation

9.   Key milestones planned for the near future include the extension of the New Deal for Communities, the introduction of the Working Families' Tax Credit, the Disabled Person's Tax Credit, Children's Tax Credit and the extension of the new pilots for access to benefit by working-age people, under the new ONE arrangements.

Bringing forward and developing new measures, in the light of work currently underway

10.   We will be taking forward work arising from the Social Exclusion Unit's recent reports on teenage pregnancies and cross-government work on care-leavers. We plan to publish White Papers on Urban and Rural Policy and a Green Paper on Housing. We will be taking forward our agenda on

neighbourhood renewal, acting on the reports from the Policy Action Teams looking at the range of problems affecting deprived neighbourhoods – from jobs and skills issues, to neighbourhood and housing management and access to financial services and shops.

Constantly reviewing, evaluating and, where necessary, adapting policies to ensure they achieve the maximum effect

11. Many of the measures set out in this report – including the Sure Start strategy, Employment Zones, Education Action and Health Action Zones, and Better Government models of delivering services for pensioners – are being piloted to test their value and to ensure that we find the best ways of designing and delivering services.

12. The indicators set out in the report will enable us to monitor progress. We will continue to develop and add to the indicators to ensure they are relevant to the task, reflecting best practice and developing thinking in the field of social exclusion. We know that there are gaps in our ability to assess and understand the impact of our policies, particularly at local level. The Social Exclusion Unit is looking at the best ways of obtaining good-quality information relating to small areas, and the Department of the Environment, Transport and the Regions is reviewing and improving its Index of Local Deprivation. Similar work is being undertaken in Scotland, Northern Ireland and Wales.

13. Our goals can only be achieved by working together effectively at both national and local levels. Devolution offers us an added chance of learning from the experiences of different countries in the UK in tackling some very similar problems.

14. If you would like further information on our strategy to tackle poverty and social exclusion please write to the following address.

The Poverty and Social Exclusion Team
Department of Social Security
1–11 John Adam Street
London WC2N 6HT

You can also use the following e-mail address:

pov@ms42.dss.gsi.gov.uk

2 THE GOVERNMENT'S STRATEGY

1 Sykes R, and Leather R, 1997, *Grey Matters: A survey of older people in England*, Anchor Trust.

2 Home Office, 1998, *British Crime Survey,* Government Statistical Service.

3 Walker A, 1993, *Age and Attitudes: Main Results from a Eurobarometer Survey*, Anchor Trust.

4 Office for National Statistics, June 1999, *Labour Force Survey Spring 1998* in *Labour Market Trends,* The Stationery Office.

5 Analysis of Households Below Average Income, Analytical Services Division, Department of Social Security.

6 Jenkins SP, 1999, *Income Dynamics in Britain 1991–96*, in *Persistent Poverty and Lifetime Inequality: The Evidence*, CASE and Her Majesty's Treasury.

7 Drever F, and Whitehead M (eds), 1997, *Health Inequalities*, Decennial Supplement, Office for National Statistics and The Stationery Office.

8 Gallie D, 1987, *The Household and Community Survey*.

9 Institute of Manpower Studies, 1993, *Basic Skills Needed at Work,* Adult Literacy and Basic Skills Unit.

10 Department of Social Security, 1998, *Households Below Average Income: A Statistical Analysis 1979–1996/97,* Corporate Data Services.

11 Parsons S, and Bynner J, 1998, *Influences on adult basic skills: factors affecting the development of literacy and numeracy from birth to age 37,* Basic Skills Agency.

12 Gosling A, Machin S, and Meghir C, 1996, *What has happened to the wages of men since 1968,* in *New Inequalities*, John Hills (ed), Cambridge University Press.

13 Department of Social Security, 1998, *Households Below Average Income: A Statistical Analysis 1979–1996/97,* Corporate Data Services.

14 Hobcraft J, 1998, *Intergenerational and life-course transmission of social exclusion: influences of childhood poverty, family disruption, and contact with the police*, CASE paper 15, London School of Economics.

15 Shropshire J, and Middleton S, 1999, *Small expectations: Learning to be poor?*, Joseph Rowntree Foundation.

16 The Scottish Office, 1999, *Social Inclusion: Opening the door to a better Scotland*.

17 Drever F, and Whitehead M (eds), 1997, *Health Inequalities*, Decennial Supplement, Office for National Statistics and The Stationery Office.

18 Department of the Environment, Transport and the Regions, 1998, *English House Condition Survey 1996,* The Stationery Office.

19 Scottish Homes, 1997, *Scottish House Condition Survey 1996*.

20 Smith G, 1999, *Area based Initiative: the rationale and options for area targeting*, CASE paper 25, London School of Economics; and Social Exclusion Unit, 1999, *Bringing Britain together: a national strategy for neighbourhood renewal (Cm 4045)*, The Stationery Office.

21 Power A, 1999, *Area Problems and Multiple Deprivation* in *Persistent Poverty and Lifetime Inequality: The Evidence,* CASE and Her Majesty's Treasury.

22 Social Exclusion Unit, 1999, *Bringing Britain together: a national strategy for neighbourhood renewal (Cm 4045)*, The Stationery Office.

23 Social Exclusion Unit, 1999, *Bringing Britain together: a national strategy for neighbourhood renewal (Cm 4045)*, The Stationery Office.

24 Social Exclusion Unit, 1999, *Bringing Britain together: a national strategy for neighbourhood renewal (Cm 4045)*, The Stationery Office.

25 Mirrlees-Black, and Allen J, 1998, *Concern about crime: findings from the 1998 British Crime Survey*, Research Findings no 83, Home Office.

26 Department of Social Security, 1998, *Households Below Average Income: A Statistical Analysis, 1979–1996/97,* Corporate Data Services.

27 Office for National Statistics, 1999, *Labour Force Survey Spring 1999* in *Labour Market Trends,* The Stationery Office.

28 Department of Social Security, 1998, *Households Below Average Income: A Statistical Analysis, 1979–1996/97,* Corporate Data Services.

29 Office for National Statistics, May 1999, *Labour Force Survey Spring 1998* in *Labour Market Trends,* The Stationery Office.

30 Analysis of the cross benefit database, Analytical Services Division, Department of Social Security. Note: Out of work benefits defined as Income Support, Jobseeker's Allowance, Incapacity Benefit and Severe Disability Allowance.

31 Stewart MB, 1999, *Low pay, no pay dynamics*, in *Persistent Poverty and Lifetime Inequality: The Evidence,* CASE and Her Majesty's Treasury.

32 Gosling A, Machin S, and Meghir C, 1996, *What has happened to the wages of men since 1968,* in *New Inequalities,* John Hills (ed), Cambridge University Press.

33 Office for National Statistics, various years, *General Household Survey,* The Stationery Office.

34 Department for Education and Employment, 1999, *National Curriculum Assessments of 7-, 11- and 14-year-olds in England,* The Stationery Office.

35 For further discussion see: Social Exclusion Unit, 1999, *Bringing Britain together: a national strategy for neighbourhood renewal (Cm 4045)*, The Stationery Office.

36 Organisation for Economic Co-operation and Development, 1998, *Employment Outlook*.

37 Social Exclusion Unit, 1999, *Teenage Pregnancy* (Cm 4342), The Stationery Office.

38 Social Exclusion Unit, 1999, *Bridging the Gap: New Opportunities for 16–18-year-olds not in Education, Employment or Training* (Cm 4405), The Stationery Office.

39 Her Majesty's Treasury, December 1998, *Public Services for the Future: Modernisation, reform, accountability* (Cm 4181), The Stationery Office.

3 CHILDREN AND YOUNG PEOPLE

1 Department of Social Security, 1998, *Households Below Average Income: A Statistical Analysis 1979–1996/97*, Corporate Data Services.

2 Department of Social Security, 1998, *Households Below Average Income: A Statistical Analysis 1979–1996/97*, Corporate Data Services.

3 Analysis based on Households Below Average Income data, Analytical Services Division, Department of Social Security.

4 Office for National Statistics, 1999, *Labour Force Survey*.

5 Analysis of the cross benefit database, Analytical Services Division, Department of Social Security. Note: Out of work benefits defined as Income Support, Jobseeker's Allowance, Incapacity Benefit and Severe Disability Allowance.

6 CASE, London School of Economics, 1999, *Persistent Poverty and Lifetime Inequality: The Evidence*, Her Majesty's Treasury.

7 Department for Education and Employment, 1999, *National Curriculum Assessments of 7-, 11- and 14-year-olds in England*, The Stationery Office.

8 Social Exclusion Unit, 1998, *Bringing Britain together: a national strategy for neighbourhood renewal* (Cm 4045), The Stationery Office.

9 Drever F, and Whitehead M (eds), 1997, *Health Inequalities*, Decennial Supplement, Office for National Statistics and The Stationery Office.

10 Department of Health, 1999, *Saving Lives: Our Healthier Nation* (Cm 4386), The Stationery Office.

11 Department of Health, 1999, *Saving Lives: Our Healthier Nation* (Cm 4386), The Stationery Office.

12 Department of Health, 1999, *Saving Lives: Our Healthier Nation* (Cm 4386), The Stationery Office.

13 Department of the Environment, Transport and the Regions, 1998, *English House Condition Survey 1996*, The Stationery Office.

14 Charlton J, and Murray M (eds), 1997, *The Health of Adult Britain 1841–1994,* Office for National Statistics.

15 Roberts, and Power, 1996, *Does the decline in child injury mortality vary by social class? A comparison of specific mortality in 1981–1991,* British Medical Journal, Vol 313.

16 Department of Health, 1999, *Saving Lives: Our Healthier Nation* (Cm 4386), The Stationery Office.

17 Social Exclusion Unit, 1999, *Teenage Pregnancy* (Cm 4342), The Stationery Office.

18 Social Exclusion Unit, 1999, *Teenage Pregnancy* (Cm 4342), The Stationery Office.

19 Department for Education and Employment press notice, 451/98.

20 Analysis based on Households Below Average Income data, Analytical Services Division, Department of Social Security.

21 Hobcraft J, 1998, *Intergenerational and life-course transmission of social exclusion: influences of childhood poverty, family disruption, and contact with the police*, CASE paper 15, London School of Economics.

22 Machin S, 1999, *Childhood Disadvantage and Intergenerational Transmission of Economic Status* in *Persistent Poverty and Lifetime Inequality: The Evidence*, CASE and Her Majesty's Treasury.

23 Johnson P, and Reed H, 1996, *Intergenerational Mobility among the Rich and Poor: results from the NCDS*, Oxford Review of Economic Policy (12.1).

24 Office for National Statistics Longitudinal Survey Analysis as quoted in *Tackling Poverty and Social Exclusion,* March 1999, Her Majesty's Treasury, Manor Park Press.

25 Feinstein L, 1998, *Pre-school Educational Inequality? British Children in the 1970 Cohort*, Centre for Economic Performance.

26 Youth Cohort Study, England 1998.

27 Hobcraft J, 1998, *Intergenerational and life-course transmission of social exclusion: influences of childhood poverty, family disruption, and contact with the police*, CASE paper 15, London School of Economics.

28 Gregg P, and Machin S, 1998, *Child Development and Success and Failure in the Youth Labour Market*, Centre for Economic Performance.

29 Social Exclusion Unit, 1999, *Teenage Pregnancy* (Cm 4342), The Stationery Office.

30 Social Exclusion Unit, 1999, *Bridging the Gap: New Opportunities for 16–18-year-olds not in Education, Employment or Training* (Cm 4405), The Stationery Office.

31 Social Exclusion Unit, 1999, *Bridging the Gap: New Opportunities for 16–18-year-olds not in Education, Employment or Training* (Cm 4405), The Stationery Office.

32 Johnson P, and Reed H, 1996, *Intergenerational Mobility among the Rich and Poor: results from the NCDS*, Oxford Review of Economic Policy (12.1).

33 Shropshire J, and Middleton S, 1999, *Small expectations: Learning to be poor?,* Joseph Rowntree Foundation.

34 Social Exclusion Unit, 1999, *Teenage Pregnancy* (Cm 4342), The Stationery Office.

35 Department for Education and Employment press notice, 272/99.

36 Department of Social Security, 1998, *Households Below Average Income: A Statistical Analysis 1979–1996/97,* Corporate Data Services.

37 Analysis based on the *Labour Force Survey,* Analytical Services Division, Department of Social Security.

4 PEOPLE OF WORKING AGE

1 Office for National Statistics, May 1999, *Labour Force Survey Spring 1998* in *Labour Market Trends,* The Stationery Office.

2 Organisation for Economic Co-operation and Development, 1998, *Employment Outlook.*

3 Jenkins SP, 1999, *Income Dynamics in Britain 1991–96,* in *Persistent Poverty and Lifetime Inequality: The Evidence,* CASE and Her Majesty's Treasury.

4 Elam and Thomas, 1997, *Stepping Stones to Employment, DSS Research report 71,* The Stationery Office.

5 Analysis of the cross benefit database, Analytical Services Division, Department of Social Security. Note: Out of work benefits defined as Income Support, Jobseeker's Allowance, Incapacity Benefit and Severe Disability Allowance.

6 1997, *Employment Opportunity in a Changing Labour Market,* Her Majesty's Treasury.

7 Gregg P, *Scarring effects of unemployment 1999* in *Persistent Poverty and Lifetime Inequality: The Evidence,* CASE and Her Majesty's Treasury.

8 Stewart MB, 1999, *Low pay, no pay dynamics,* 1999, in *Persistent Poverty and Lifetime Inequality: The Evidence,* CASE and Her Majesty's Treasury.

9 Gregg P, *Scarring effects of unemployment 1999* in *Persistent Poverty and Lifetime Inequality: The Evidence,* CASE and Her Majesty's Treasury.

10 Parsons S, and Bynner J, 1998, *Influences on adult basic skills: factors affecting the development of literacy and numeracy from birth to age 37,* Basic Skills Agency. Note: based on the National Child Development Study – birth cohort born in 1958.

11 Organisation for Economic Co-operation and Development, 1997, *Literacy Skills for the Knowledge Society.*

12 Department of Social Security, 1998, *Households Below Average Income, A Statistical Analysis 1979–1996/97,* Corporate Data Services.

13 Shaw A, Walker R, Jenkins S, and Middleton S, 1996, *Moving off Income Support: barriers and bridges*, DSS Research Report.

14 Bottomley, McKay and Walker, 1995, *Unemployment and Jobseeking*, DSS Research Report No. 62, The Stationery Office.

15 Bottomley, McKay and Walker, 1997, *Unemployment and Jobseeking*, DSS Research Report No. 62, The Stationery Office.

16 Bottomley, McKay and Walker, 1997, *Unemployment and Jobseeking*, DSS Research Report No. 62, The Stationery Office.

17 Elias P, 1997, *The Effect of Unemployment Benefits on the labour force participation of partners*, Institute of Employment.

18 Office for National Statistics, 1999, *Labour Force Survey Summer 1998*. A person is defined as having a current, long term disability if they have a disability which limits the kind or amount of work they can do, or has a substantial impact on their day-to-day activities, or is known to have a progressive condition.

19 Campbell N, 1999, *The decline in employment among older people in Britain*, CASE paper 19, London School of Economics.

20 Office for National Statistics, 1999, *Labour Force Survey*. Note: average spring 1998 to winter 1998/9.

21 Office for National Statistics, 1999, *Labour Force Survey*. Note: average 1996–1998.

22 Analysis of Family and Working Lives Survey by RSL Marketing and Social Research Ltd for Department for Education and Employment.

23 Social Exclusion Unit, July 1998, *Rough Sleeping* (CM 4008), The Stationery Office.

24 Analytical Services Division, Department of Social Security.

25 Analysis of the cross benefit database, Analytical Services Division, Department of Social Security. Note: Out of work benefits defined as Income Support, Jobseeker's Allowance, Incapacity Benefit and Severe Disability Allowance.

26 Her Majesty's Treasury, 1999, *Financial Statement and Budget Report*, The Stationery Office.

27 Parsons S, and Bynner J, 1998, *Influences on adult basic skills: factors affecting the development of literacy and numeracy from birth to age 37,* Basic Skills Agency. Note: based on the National Child Development Study – birth cohort born in 1958.

28 Department of Health, 1999, *Saving Lives: Our Healthier Nation* (Cm 4386), The Stationery Office.

5 OLDER PEOPLE

1 Department of Social Security, 1999, *The Pensioners' Incomes Series 1996/97,* Government Statistical Service.

2 Office for National Statistics, 1999, *Social Focus on Older People,* Government Statistical Service.

3 Acheson, 1998, *Independent Inquiry into Inequalities in Health,* The Stationery Office.

4 Department of Social Security, 1998, *Households Below Average Income: A Statistical Analysis 1979–1995/96,* Corporate Data Services.

5 Department of Social Security, 1999, *The Pensioners' Incomes Series 1996/97*, Government Statistical Service.

6 Department of the Environment, Transport and the Regions, 1998, *English House Condition Survey 1996*, The Stationery Office.

7 Department of the Environment, Transport and the Regions, 1999, *Fuel Poverty: The new Home Energy Efficiency Scheme – a programme for warmer, healthier homes*.

8 Sykes R, and Leather R, 1997, *Grey Matters: A survey of older people in England*, Anchor Trust.

9 Office for National Statistics, 1999, *Social Trends 29,* The Stationery Office.

10 Disney R, Grundy E, and Johnson P, 1997, *The Dynamics of Retirement*, The Stationery Office.

11 Office for National Statistics, 1999, *Social Trends 29,* The Stationery Office.

12 Acheson, 1998, *Independent Inquiry into Inequalities in Health*, The Stationery Office.

13 Sykes R, and Leather R, 1997, *Grey Matters: A survey of older people in England,* Anchor Trust.

14 Department of Health, 1999, *Saving Lives: Our Healthier Nation* (Cm 4386), The Stationery Office.

15 Home Office, 1998, *British Crime Survey*, Government Statistical Service.

16 Analysis of *Family Resources Survey 1997/98,* Analytical Services Division, Department of Social Security.

17 Analysis of *Family Resources Survey 1997/98,* Analytical Services Division, Department of Social Security.

18 Analysis based on a 5 per cent sample of the Pension Strategy Computer System, Analytical Services Division, Department of Social Security.

19 Fuel Poverty – a fuel-poor household is defined as one which needs to spend in excess of 10 per cent of income on fuel to maintain a satisfactory heating regime.

6 COMMUNITIES

1 Office for National Statistics, January 1999, *Labour Force Survey Spring 1998* in *Labour Market Trends,* The Stationery Office.

2 Smith GR, May 1999, *Area-based Initiatives: the rationale for and options for targeting*, CASE paper 25, London School of Economics.

3 The Scottish Office, 1999, *Social Inclusion: Opening the door to a better Scotland*.

4 Power A, 1999, *Area Problems and Multiple Deprivation* in *Persistent Poverty and Lifetime Inequality: The Evidence*, CASE and Her Majesty's Treasury.

5 Kleinman M, 1998, *Include Me Out ? The New Politics of Place and Poverty*, CASE paper 11, London School of Economics.

6 Socio-spatial Analysis Research Unit (SARU), 1997, *Urban Labour Markets in the Belfast Urban Area*, The Queen's University of Belfast.

7 Smith GR, May 1999, *Area-based Initiatives: the rationale for and options for targeting*, CASE paper 25, London School of Economics. Note: figures relates to August 1996 before the introduction of Jobseeker's Allowance.

8 Department of Education Northern Ireland (DENI), Annual School Census 1998/99.

9 Social Exclusion Unit, 1998, *Bringing Britain together: a national strategy for neighbourhood renewal* (Cm 4045), The Stationery Office.

10 Welsh Office, March 1999, *Building an Inclusive Wales: Tackling the Social Exclusion Agenda*.

11 The Scottish Office, 1999, *Social Inclusion: Opening the door to a better Scotland*.

12 Social Exclusion Unit, 1998, *Bringing Britain together: a national strategy for neighbourhood renewal* (Cm 4045), The Stationery Office.

13 Social Exclusion Unit, 1998, *Bringing Britain together: a national strategy for neighbourhood renewal* (Cm 4045), The Stationery Office.

14 Department of the Environment, Transport and the Regions, 1998, *English House Condition Survey 1996*, The Stationery Office.

15 Social Exclusion Unit, 1998, *Bringing Britain together: a national strategy for neighbourhood renewal* (Cm 4045), The Stationery Office.

16 Figures based on data supplied by General Registrars Office Northern Ireland, 1996.

17 The Scottish Office, 1999, *Social Inclusion: Opening the door to a better Scotland*.

18 Welsh Office, March 1999, *Building an Inclusive Wales: Tackling the Social Exclusion Agenda*.

19 Social Exclusion Unit, 1998, *Bringing Britain together: a national strategy for neighbourhood renewal* (Cm 4045), The Stationery Office.

20 Social Exclusion Unit, 1998, *Bringing Britain together: a national strategy for neighbourhood renewal* (Cm 4045), The Stationery Office.

21 Department of Social Security, 1999, *Family Resources Survey 1997/98,* Corporate Data Services.

22 Whyley C, McCormick J and Kempson E, 1998, *Paying for peace of mind: access to home contents insurance for low-income households*, Policy Studies Institute.

23 The Scottish Office, 1999, *Social Inclusion: Opening the door to a better Scotland*.

24 Social Exclusion Unit, 1998, *Bringing Britain together: a national strategy for neighbourhood renewal* (Cm 4045), The Stationery Office.

25 Taylor M, 1995, *Unleashing the potential: bringing residents to the centre of regeneration*, Joseph Rowntree Foundation.

26 Power A and Munford K, 1999, *The slow death of great cities? Urban abandonment or urban renaissance,* Joseph Rowntree Foundation.

27 Power A, 1996, *Area-based poverty, social problems and resident empowerment*, London School of Economics/STICERO.

28 Power A, 1996, *Area-based poverty, social problems and resident empowerment*, London School of Economics/STICERO.

29 Gallie D, 1987, *The Household and Community Survey*.